TH SECOND TOWER'S DOWN

John McCole

ROBSON
BOOKS

First published in Great Britain in 2002 by Robson Books,
64 Brewery Road, London N7 9NY

A member of **Chrysalis** Books plc

British Library Cataloguing in Publication Data
A catalogue record for this title is available from the British
Library.

ISBN 1 86105 576 5

Typeset in 11.5/14pt Times by FiSH Books, London WC1
Printed by Creative Print & Design (Wales), Ebbw Vale

Dedication:

To my wife and my children,
who have helped me more than they know.

To my parents and family,
who have always been there for me.

To the New York firefighters who are left to carry on,
despite the memories that they bear.

To the 343 guys who will never hear the
tone alarm call again.

You will never be forgotten.

Contents

Acknowledgements   vii

Map   ix

Introduction   1

Prologue   3

1   September 11   7

2   Going to Work   19

3   The Day After   48

4   September 13/14   60

5   The Bucket Brigades   80

6   The World Trade Center Task Force   96

7   Day Two with Engine 37   103

8   Day Tour in Midtown   112

9   Eddy Day's Memorial   119

10   Night Tour on 29th Street   124

11   Toxic Fire   134

12   Dealing with Anthrax   140

13   Addressing My Health   143

14   Fire's in the Mind   152

15   Getting Healthy   157

16   After September 11   164

Acknowledgements

There are many people who have helped me since the attacks of September 11, including those who also played a crucial part in my life before that date. Thanks especially to the following persons and groups:

The staff of Celebrity Center, NYC, for their dedication to making the world a better place to live – especially the technical delivery team, who have stood by me throughout the last nine months.

The Health Med clinic, Sacramento, California – especially Keith Miller, Dr David Root and James Woodworth – for their delivery of the Hubbard Purification Program, and their efforts to serve all those who participated in the Ground Zero rescue and recovery.

Bruce Montigney, for the computer wizardry that frequently bailed me out in the middle of the night. Shirlee Montigney, for her guidance and literary advice.

Kelly McClosky, for her administrative help and cooperation.

Jayne Kraman, for helping me to get through the whole ordeal in spite of myself.

And, not least, my mom, for her contribution and administrative assistance.

Special thanks also to the following, who made publication of this book possible:

The New York Fire Department, which carries on despite all its losses. While the ranks are decimated, the men and women serving on the front line and working in administration have shown a New York spirit that should inspire the whole world.

Grant Hudson, Professor of English, for all his help in the creation of this book.

Paul Woods, an author and journalist whose editorial guidance helped present a story that might otherwise have been difficult to tell.

James Hunt, whose guidance and assistance reassured me that my interests, and the integrity of the FDNY, would be well protected.

Bob Keenan, a veteran firefighter in London, who put the idea into my head as we were leaving the site of Ground Zero. He has supported me as only another firefighter could, in helping to put forward *our* side of the story.

All of the guys named above made a significant contribution to this book, and have ensured that the firefighters of New York are honoured in a manner that they truly deserve.

I would like to make a special dedication to the late L Ron Hubbard, for his researching and development of the detoxification programme that I believe has extended my life. It's to him I owe the knowledge that I will still be around in the days ahead – to continue in my job as a New York firefighter, and to watch my baby boy grow up, perhaps to follow one day in his father's footsteps.

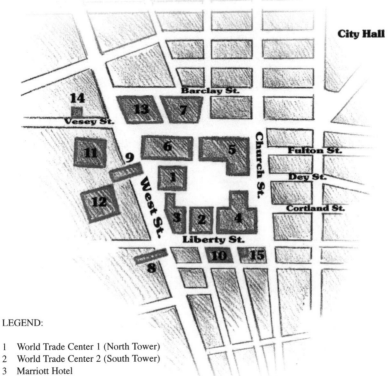

City Hall

Barclay St.

Vesey St.

Church St.

Fulton St.

Dey St.

West St.

Cortland St.

Liberty St.

LEGEND:

1   World Trade Center 1 (North Tower)
2   World Trade Center 2 (South Tower)
3   Marriott Hotel
4   World Trade Center 4
5   World Trade Center 5
6   World Trade Center 6
7   World Trade Center 7
8   Liberty St. Walkway
9   Vesey St. Walkway
10 Bankers' Trust
11 World Financial Center 3
12 World Financial Center 2
13 Verizon Building
14 Tex-mex Restaurant
15 Firehouse

Introduction

My name is John McCole, and I am a New York City fire lieutenant. I've been on the job for eighteen years, most of it spent in busy areas of Manhattan and Brooklyn. My father was a NYC fireman and so was my uncle. My sister is married to a firefighter, who is one of the many friends I've made while being on the job. My cousin is a fireman. So you could say, it sort of runs in the family.

I've been a lieutenant for the past five years. After the World Trade Center disaster, I was drawn to find out exactly what went on that day. There's something about remembering all the details of an event such as this that helps one to get past it. It's not knowing exactly what happened that keeps one's attention fixed on the past. I lost a lot of guys that I had worked with throughout the years and, everywhere I went, their friends had stories to tell.

In the beginning, everybody was talking about what happened. In fact, it seemed like all I was hearing were horror stories of September 11. It was utterly overwhelming.

As time has gone on, I've noticed that firefighters have backed off from talking about it. Some of the guys I've spoken with have forgotten a lot of what took place, they say. To ease my grief, I started to write down what happened that day and in the days and weeks that followed. I felt that with each passing week, I'd lose my memory of that day's terrible events.

As what I wrote began to take form, I was urged by many of my friends to turn it into a book. This is my account of what happened on that day, as well as the days and weeks that followed, and what I did to help myself both physically and spiritually.

As a covering officer, which means I'm not permanently assigned to any firehouse in particular, I had the unusual experience of working in many of the firehouses that suffered from heavy casualties. I've had an interesting life and have tried to blend this with the story of 9/11.

Despite everything it's a story of hope. I've tried to convey to the reader that something can be done to improve our world, to maybe make it a better place to live...for everyone.

John McCole

Prologue

Shooting down 79th Street, under the overpass heading west, I can see a traffic circle in front of the firetruck – beyond that is the Hudson River. Our way is clear.

'Go to the left!' I holler.

I push back into my seat, crammed in between the front seats and the back windows.

We swerve left and I hit the door. It knocks the wind out of me. We're taking the quickest way around the circle, against the incoming traffic lane, and I can feel the whole truck straining to the left with the occasional shudder as it hits a pothole. I grip the leather seat and put my hand on the ceiling, so as to stabilise myself and keep from falling over. It was already a rough ride.

I can hear the trailer hitch clanking on the stiff turns, and it sounds like it might become detached. I'm expecting all the horns to sound as we drive into a sea of cars, but there isn't any traffic. Not one solitary vehicle. It's like a ghost town.

All the time I'm thinking about how to cut down our journey time to the World Trade Center. But there's also an unspoken apprehension, a sense that, while this is something we've been trained for, it may not be like anything else we've seen. Every curve of the road, every short cut, every traffic violation we make only seems to extend our journey. My watch seems to have slowed down and everything is taking for ever. But I look to the left, and see that the highway leading downtown is deserted.

My alertness and anticipation had fed into a kind of excitement, but now it's become a fear of seeing what nobody should ever have to see.

Our driver, John Paul, steers the pick-up between two police cars as they back up. They've been stationed to block any traffic from coming through and it looks like we're the first rescue services on their route. The squad cars rock in the wind as the pick-up surges through the gap. Heavy tools in a bag near my feet come loose and whack my bare shins. Fuck! That hurt! John bounces the rig up the entrance ramp to the remainder of the Henry Hudson Parkway, which turns into West Street just a mile or so south, and then continues straight down to the World Trade Center. Behind us, I feel the decontamination trailer swinging around as we make the turn – if we move too fast it'll overturn, so I look in the rear-view mirror to make sure it's still there.

Just before we hit the highway I see a stop sign. Police have closed all traffic lanes along the parkway, so John Paul barely slows, thundering out on to the highway. All the emergency services are playing everything by the book. Just like it said in the books when I was studying to become a fire lieutenant many years ago. They didn't write any book for what we were all about to encounter in the few brief moments that were to follow, however.

As we head down the parkway, I can hear a lot of fragmented reports coming in on the truck radio. Much of what we hear is hard to make out. The first tower fell at 9.48 a.m., just as we were leaving, and we have no idea of what it's like down there. We don't know how many of our brothers managed to get the hell out, or how many remain buried inside. All we have are these jumbled words blurting out of the speaker.

Out of the muddle of static, I can make out a single voice: a firefighter who's trapped and has nowhere to go. He says he can't breathe, and doesn't think he's going to make it. The truck he's trapped in is filling up with smoke. He's pleading with the dispatcher for help.

All we can do is listen.

After I'd heard the first tower had fallen, I felt numbed. My mind already feels hazed, as though part of my memory has been blacked out. I watched it all coming down on the TV set at the firehouse, but told myself that there must be at least forty to fifty storeys still standing... surely? But then again, I'd watched those little dark shapes falling from the building and was trying to identify where they were coming from. It wasn't until the commentator spoke that I finally recognised the shapes as people, jumping for their lives. Jumping hundreds of feet to certain death. The whole thing has me so horrified that I'm not currently certain of what I have and haven't seen.

I remember getting into the rig as we left the firehouse, saying to the guys, 'How can this be?' The World Trade Center has been the most recognisable feature of lower Manhattan's financial district for more than 25 years, longer than I've been a firefighter. Now we're bracing ourselves to see it brought down in a flaming mesh of concrete and steel. It's just unreal.

In the cab, the guys are handling the news in different ways, all fighting their own private battles with the reality of it. 'Man, there's going to be a lot of fire for everyone,' I'm thinking to myself, and wondering if we already lost some guys when the tower came down.

Making our way down the parkway towards West Street, I can see the cloud of smoke and dust that's billowing up from the towers. The cloud has to be close to two thousand feet in the air, a giant, grey, distorted blur. I can't see the towers at all, but then the cloud is blocking them out.

We get to the crest of the highway, and I hand my camera to John Hunt, for him to snap off a few shots. The smoke continues to rise, and we have no idea of what we're driving into. None of us have seen anything like this before.

At the same time, none of us should be feeling such a fear of the unknown. At any time during a tour of duty, we can be woken up at three in the morning to rush to a burning tenement. Once there, we see people bailing out from several storeys above. So why should any of this seem new to us? We should have been conditioned to get used to it by now. But, after seventeen years on the job, I know that today is going to be an exceptionally bad day.

A cop waves us on from the side of the street, the rest of the traffic totally blocked off. Cops are all over the place. They look as bewildered as we feel, stumbling through a slow-moving nightmare. The people who are moved on from the scene show no signs of wanting to come any further south. They have the right idea. Some of them look relieved at seeing us pass, as if the cavalry has arrived. I wish I could agree.

The streets are in the low fifties now. Speeding down off the highway on to West Street, businesspeople are walking north with their heads down, shuffling forward like a line of beaten soldiers. Dazed and pan-faced, they seem at least as mystified as we are by what's happened.

Down around the forties, there's an unstoppable flow of people walking north. It's quiet in the cab of the pick-up. Each of us seems alone in his own head. On West Street, I see the enormous cloud that's been out of our sight for about a minute. I tell John to take some more shots – I don't know why. The cloud has got bigger, and darker, and now, on what started as a clear, bright September morning, has blocked out the sun.

In the twenties now. Another thirty blocks or so to go and we'll be there. I can already smell the World Trade Center burning. It isn't like your normal everyday tenement fire, which is mostly burning wood – from this distance it's like a fire at a garbage dump, man-made materials like plastic, polystyrene and pressboard burning with a steely, metallic, electrical stench that underpins it all.

People are still streaming past us, and a lot of these folks are covered with some kind of white powder. It's as if the twin towers opened up like clouds, and delivered a metallic snowstorm. Greyer and far more ominous than natural snow, it seems to wrap the financial district in a blanket of silence.

Outside, beyond the dark cloud, it's still a nice day, sunny and fresh. With the sun still shining, it's probably a good day for those folks out on the northern shores of Long Island who haven't heard what's happened yet, guys trying to grab that one last day at the beach.

Less than two minutes away from the World Trade Center, a voice comes on the radio from a guy who's right there in the thick of it.

'The second tower's down! The second tower's down...'

Then the radio goes dead. The silence seems to last for ever. All of us in the pick-up know what we're up against now. We all know that firemen must have been in the tower, and deep down we know what must have happened to them.

1

September 11

I live in Spanish Harlem, about twenty blocks north of the Upper East Side of Manhattan. (Sometimes known as the *upper* Upper East Side.) It's not the best part of town, and the streets are always dirty – even after the street sweeper comes by. There are a lot of rundown or boarded-up buildings in our area, but lately there's been a real-estate resurgence and vacant buildings are starting to be renovated. At the rate it's going, in ten years this neighbourhood will become a really nice place to live.

It's been a constantly changing neighbourhood for the last fifty years, and there are more ethnic groups here than I've ever known or lived with before. I get along with all my neighbours. There's an old black guy named Charlie, who helps out the Italian carpenter whose backyard runs into our own. We've got to know each other pretty well, and sometimes go fishing together down on the East River. There's a 'bodega' every block – their name taken from the Spanish word for a ship's store or stronghold, these family stores sell everything from soup to nuts. It helps if you know some Spanish around here, and I've been learning a little for the last three years. The local Puerto Rican people have reclaimed a lot of the vacant land where buildings used to stand. They usually put up a little shack, then grow some vegetables. On the weekends, the men gather there to talk, play dominoes and drink, which I guess is what they did back home. Some even keep chickens, and I hear the call of a rooster once in a while.

It's a tough place. Drugs are very prevalent, and at night you see people coming and going on the corners where heroin and crack are

7

sold. Every once in a while, I'll come around the corner and the plain-clothes cops have everyone down on their faces, spreadeagled in a drug bust. A couple of days later, someone new takes the place of whoever got busted. The junkies all leave me alone. I know where they're coming from, and I won't take any shit from them. As long as they keep to their own space, then everything is cool. They've been there for the last forty years and I don't expect they'll be leaving anytime soon. Not until the neighbourhood changes, anyway.

It was my wife's idea to move up here, after seeing an ad for an apartment for rent. When I saw the address, my initial response was, 'No fucking way, I ain't living *there*.' However, my wife has her street smarts, having grown up in the city. She's also a very persistent young lady – seven years younger than me, in the prime of her early thirties as I was hitting forty – so I went to look at the place.

Straight away, it had an old world charm that grabbed me. It reminded me of when I was young and growing up on Staten Island, where the pace of life is a lot slower than that of Manhattan. It was an old Italian neighbourhood, at one time full of tenements and brownstones. Some blocks are still intact and kept very nicely, but they're the exception. One such is our own apartment block, which has a backyard with grape vines and fig trees that looks like it's straight out of the fifties.

Our yard has a mulberry tree, a crab-apple tree and climbing ivy. We even put in a small fishpond, complete with a miniature waterfall, a few grape vines and a trellis that offers a little privacy out there. It makes me laugh when the neighbours call from their tenement windows to say how nice everything is looking, as if I'm some kind of expert gardener.

When we moved in I had grand plans for a nice little vegetable garden, but too little sun falls on the yard every day. When things did start to grow, the birds quickly reduced it all down to nothing. As for fruits, it's less hassle to buy them from the local store. But I look forward to spending time in that garden, especially in the summer after a hard stint at the firehouse. When everybody's hanging out on the stoops with their music blasting, I open the door to my yard and it's like I'm somewhere else. It sure doesn't feel like the city.

I've lived there since March of 1999. The rent is low, we can always park our car, and I'm not more than ten minutes away from the Upper East Side, so I guess I can call it home.

The morning of September 11 2001 started early for me, around 7 a.m. Leaving my wife and our little boy sleeping, I'd slipped out into the backyard for a few minutes before heading off to do some volunteer work at the church I belong to. It was a beautiful beginning to the day – sunny, mild, fresh. I took a look around the garden at all the things I hadn't got around to doing that summer, and then headed out to the concrete jungle.

The traffic didn't seem too bad, so there was time to pick up a coffee. I caught all the green lights on Second Avenue and turned right on to 81st Street. The church was just three blocks from the coffee shop, so I had just enough time to make it.

As I pulled up in front of the building where the church is located, I heard a report on the radio: 'We're getting disturbing reports of a fire on the upper floors of the World Trade Center.' I knew then that some of the guys were going to be busy. Any fire can be a living nightmare, but high-rise fires are a whole different animal.

It was 8.55 a.m.

Nothing whatsoever was said about an airplane. The idea that the cause was a plane crashing into the north tower, rather than an internal fire, or even arson, would have seemed too wild to be true at first. However, had I known, I'd probably have headed for the nearest firehouse; then, when the second plane hit, I'd have been down there in a heartbeat.

But that's all that was said, strange as it seems. I thought, 'Man, that's gonna be one really tough job. Hopefully it'll burn itself out before they even get up there.' I'd walked up to the 42nd floor back in '93, after the WTC bombing. It took us about twenty minutes and all we had on was our 'turnout gear' – our coats, boots and helmets. We didn't have to bring our breathing apparatus along with us for some reason. The Self Contained Breathing Apparatus (SCBA, just a mask basically), protective pants, jacket and helmet, all combined weighs 70 pounds, which is damn heavy.

Each mask weighs about 30 pounds on its own, and consists of an air cylinder held in a harness with a mechanism that reduces the high pressure of the air, so we can breathe it through a hose attached to the face-piece. If these guys had to go to the 70th floor with all their gear, I knew they'd be shot before they even got to work. The elevators aren't always a safe bet, so they were going to have to walk up a lot of stairs.

I walked up to the fourth floor of the six-storey building, where I was supposed to be working that day.

I briefly thought that if I went to the top floor I could see anything from there. But when I got up there and looked around, I realised I was dwarfed by all the twenty- and thirty-storey luxury apartment buildings. The only thing I could see was New York's famous skyline.

It was now 9.10 a.m., and only two other volunteers had arrived. I was just about to call one of the people who was supposed to be there, when a lady who works on the floor above came in. She had a foreboding look on her face, and I thought she was going to yell at me for something.

'The World Trade Center towers have both been hit by airplanes,' she said. 'It was a terrorist attack!'

My heart began to race, just like when an emergency call came over the loudspeaker. 'You'd better call your firehouse, because there was an announcement on the radio that all off-duty firefighters were to come in.'

Recalls are put into effect when catastrophes like this happen. I made several calls to different firehouses, but all the lines were busy. I finally got through to someone at the quarters of Engine 54 and Ladder 4, a guy I'd been promoted with back in the fall of '97.

'Hey Bob, what the hell is going on?' I asked. He just launched into it.

'Man, there's like thirty floors of fire in the north tower, it's absolutely fucking incredible!'

'Was it two planes?'

'Yeah, both towers have been hit. Hey listen, this place is crazy, the other phone is ringing off the hook. Just go to your battalion – that's all I know.'

Man, it must be nuts over there, I thought. They're right in the heart of midtown and it's always crazy, now it must be like a fucking zoo.

It was 9.25 a.m. when I turned up Third Avenue towards my house. I looked downtown, through the canyons of buildings that make up the city, towards where the towers were, and could see the smoke ninety-plus blocks away. Jesus, this *is* serious, I thought. I noticed the axle was rattling pretty badly in my old 1985 Toyota Camry. One of these days the wheel was just going to fall right off – but please not *today*, at least not for the ten minutes it was going to take me to get home.

I turned on the news station. The announcer explained how smoke and flames were issuing from several floors of both towers. People were so desperate that they were jumping from the skyscraper, rather than face what was behind them. It was like something out of a horror movie. My experience allowed me to sympathise with people who'd rather fall a hundred floors than go through the flames.

I *had* to get there. I *had* to join the guys who were working their way up to the fire. I *had* to get there and help.

All the high-rise fires that I'd experienced had been bad ones. It sometimes took seven or eight attempts to get water to the fire. Firefighters took the nozzle of the hose in as far as they could, cooling off the area – but, because of all the work they'd had to do in just getting to the damn fire, they either ran out of air, or strength, or both, and had to be relieved by a fresh crew. All of this is done in pitch-black smoke and intense heat, with a lot of yelling, and shoving, and guys crawling in and out. It's the worst confusion imaginable, but the longer you've been in the Fire Department then the more you can make sense of what you're doing.

Unbeknown to me – or to most of the FDNY at that point – five floors or more of each tower had been immediately engulfed in flames ignited from the jet fuel. Each plane had an impact of more than a million tons. Each carried over 15,000 gallons of fuel. When the impact ignited the oil, the towers started burning at a temperature of at least 1,000 degrees. If I'd known that, I'd have understood that there was no way on earth this fire was going to be put out.

*

I was almost home now. As I pulled up to the front of my building, a guy named Adam, who owns the service station across the street, walked over to me. Somewhere around the block, a woman screamed at the top of her lungs. We could see the smoke rising all the way from downtown.

'You're going down there, aren't you? This is the way it is back in Israel, every day, it's crazy!'

I told him I understood what he meant, but wasn't really listening. The news was obviously spreading. I politely excused myself and told him I had to get going. He grabbed my arm and looked intently at me. 'Please be careful.' I smiled. 'Hey Adam, this is what you pay your taxes for – firefighters to go to fires.'

I headed inside to break the news to my wife. The apartment was quiet and Tami was still asleep. I went into the bedroom and gently put my hand on her leg.

'Babe? Honey, get up.'

She stirred. 'Oh, why are you waking me?'

'Something real bad has happened.' I put it as gently as I could. She sat up in bed, fully awake now.

'The World Trade Center has been hit by planes. It was a terrorist attack, there's a ton of fire down there and all off-duty firefighters are being called in for duty.'

Now she was really awake, and so was our one-year-old baby boy, Bryce.

'Mommy, mommy, mommy!' he called out, looking over the rail of his crib. I went over to pick him up and he flopped back down. He wanted his mommy. I smiled at him – he was such a mommy's boy, and his daddy was so often out working. I picked him up anyway, and put him down on the floor. He ran over to Tami.

'Do you mean you have to go down there?' She was looking right at me and I could see she wasn't too thrilled.

'There's a recall, honey, and everyone's needed. I'm going over to the battalion to see what the deal is gonna be. I've tried to call several times but no one is answering.'

It was now 9.35 a.m. I changed into my uniform, slipping my shorts on and fresh white socks.

'Honey, you have to promise me you're going to be careful. Please.'

'Sure. Of course I'll be careful.'

She looked at me. I knew she was concerned, but she didn't want to press the point. She knew what she was getting into when she married me, and she was going to have to trust me a whole lot over the next couple of days.

When I was through getting dressed, I pulled her close and gave her a good, long hug. I kissed Bryce goodbye and turned to depart. Leaving the bedroom, I saw a camera sitting fully loaded with film.

'Ah, what the hell.' I took it with me.

'I'll call you as soon as I can, promise.'

'OK. Just be careful.'

With one last look at both of them, I headed out the door.

I'd been a lieutenant for almost four years. I hadn't been assigned to a permanent firehouse yet, and usually covered for other lieutenants on vacation. So I went to a firehouse for anywhere from two to three weeks at a time, and I usually had my turnout gear in my trunk when I was in-between spots. Luckily, this was the case today.

I was only seven blocks from the battalion, which was the administrative HQ for all the companies (around five or six) that operated within that area. A 'battalion' describes a group of firehouses, or companies, in military terms. The ranks above firefighter are lieutenant, captain, battalion chief, and then deputy chief. A deputy chief is in charge of several battalions, called a 'division'. I'd been assigned to this office, but usually worked anywhere in the division. Manhattan is split up into three divisions, each consisting of several battalions. The first division starts at the southernmost tip and goes up to about the thirties, where the third division picks up and continues on to 125th Street. Everything north of 125th Street is considered to be the sixth division. My division was the third.

In this particular firehouse there were two other units, Engine 35 and Ladder 14. A ladder company – also called a truck company – is responsible for all of the heavy work such as forcing open doors, breaking windows to ventilate and searching for victims. The engine company concentrates on putting out the fire with the hose. The engine operates as a team, working together, whereas the truck members often work independently of one another. A man is either a 'truckie' or an 'engineman', and it all looks very chaotic – but, in reality, every man knows his job.

Heading back north up Third Avenue for four more blocks, I looked in the rear-view mirror and saw that the big grey cloud was growing. I stopped at a red light. The driver in the car next to me shook his head, saying, 'Man, this world is going nuts.'

I nodded. 'Yeah, now I got to go down there and clear it up.' I tried to sound cheerful. He saw the FDNY patch on my arm and smiled. 'God bless and good luck.'

The firehouse looked quiet, and I thought that perhaps the units had relocated. That's what happens when there's a big fire anywhere in the city – units from outlying areas are brought in to cover the area where the fire is, so there's protection for everyone.

As I picked up my helmet, pants and jacket I felt myself shaking slightly, partly through fear and partly through excitement. I pushed the combination buttons on the door handle and entered. The firehouse was empty. The only murmurs came from the television sets dotted around the place. All of them featured the same picture: the burning towers, a nightmare played out in multiple.

I looked at the discarded shoes that were lying there on either side of where the fire truck had been. The smell of diesel and a recent fire lingered in the air. The odour would remain, as would the shoes, but it seemed far from certain how many owners might be coming back to reclaim them.

In the kitchen there was a big TV screen placed up on high. I watched people jumping from the top floors of the towers. I knew the reality of that, and I guess I'd do the same. When you're burning up, there's nothing you can think about except getting away from the heat and the flames. If your instinct tells you to jump to avoid horrific, indescribable pain, then you jump. It was hard to watch.

I got on the phone to see who was still around. I called Engine 91, but the line was busy. I heard the front door slam open and one of the younger firefighters, James Freeley, ran past me. 'Hey Lou,' (that's what the guys call a lieutenant) was all he said as he ran upstairs to get dressed. Another guy ran in and hit the button opening the door where the chief's car was usually parked. I saw a wide red and white pick-up truck with a decontamination trailer connected to the back.

The driver was a guy named John Paul, and his buddy, John Hunt, emerged from the other side of the pick-up. These guys were assigned to Ladder 14, and had worked with me on several occasions over the past three years. Three guys itching to go into the fire, all named John. How crazy is it that I should be amused by something like that, at that very moment? But, believe me, it's trivia like this that can keep you sane during an emergency.

There was no time for small talk. I could see they intended to get down to the WTC, so I found four empty mask frames and several spare face-pieces in the office. John Hunt turned up a power saw that could be used to cut steel. John Paul had two axes and a few hooks over his shoulders, and the young guy, James, had a few spare masks complete with face-pieces.

We headed down Third Avenue the wrong way, against the traffic, for about 25 blocks, dragging this big trailer that kept us from picking up speed. Suddenly, over the radio we got the report that the first tower had collapsed. Each of us shook our head. 'How can this be?' I said, mainly to myself. 'How could it happen?'

I thought that maybe there would be floors left standing. I thought I saw it come down and that perhaps it was only a partial collapse. Guiding the trailer through the streets, we were concentrating more on avoiding an accident than on the static bursts of information from the radio.

Making a right on 97th Street we made our way through Central Park, waved on by cops who had closed the park down to all other traffic. Exiting the park, we headed down to 79th Street where there was an entrance ramp to the Henry Hudson Parkway, which would take us downtown the quickest...

As we moved down the block to the World Trade Center, people were streaming by. These folks were all covered with white dust and grey ash, every one of them. They looked like ghosts, like lost souls who didn't yet know whether they'd truly survived or not.

The right-hand lane that we were in was backed up with parked cars and emergency vehicles. It was literally impossible to go any further. John Paul decided to test the other side of the road and swerved across the oncoming traffic.

We pulled into an area that reminded me of the movie *Armageddon*. The ground was covered with fine white powder and so much paper – financial invoices, business letters, confidential tax forms strewn around like so much old confetti wherever you looked. The air was full of grey metallic ash, a hellish snowfall. I was transfixed by what I saw, but was not truly aware of what I was looking at. It was surreal.

We were driving into another world. A world that seemed silent, but actually hummed with background noise. A world transformed. A world I did not recognise.

A couple of police vans were pulling away from the kerb about a block ahead of us. As we got closer, I could see their windshield wipers pushing two to three inches of that hellish soot and dust from their front windshields.

All around us, people were bailing out. I didn't notice panic but there was something else...a kind of deadness, a disbelief as to what had happened. We drove up as far as we could and left space for another vehicle to pass. All of us got out of the pick-up. I noticed cameramen taking footage of whatever they could. It didn't seem to me that they realised the magnitude of what they were filming – but then, it was all so hard to take in.

We were about four long blocks from Vesey Street now, actually about a quarter mile north of the block where the WTC was located. I went around back to put on my turnout gear. John Hunt called over, 'Hey Lou, Engine 76 is here and they've got a whole bunch of bottles,' meaning air cylinders for our masks. Engine 76 had come down with the thawing apparatus, used for unfreezing fire hydrants in the dead of winter. They didn't have any mask harnesses, but we had enough for everyone so we all shared equipment. We started to move towards what was left of the twin towers. Two blocks from Vesey, a girl handed us some paper respirators – those disposable masks you can buy in a hardware store with a metal strip across the nose, that you mould to the shape of your face.

Walking along the uptown traffic lane, as I looked through the dust and smoke I made out a figure walking towards us. It was one of the guys who had been on the initial call. He'd obviously been there when one of the towers had come down, and was covered from head to toe in dust, ash and all kinds of crap. He was shuffling towards us like a refugee from hell. If it wasn't easy to make out whether or not he was bleeding, that was only because of the black soot that ran into his cuts. At that moment, I felt a real concern as to what we were going to find. I watched as he just slumped down on the kerb, throwing his turnout coat down on the ground. He placed his head into his hands and tried to wipe all of the shit off his face. There was nothing to say, so we carried on.

John Hunt was walking so fast that I had trouble keeping up with him. John's a tough bastard, fit too, with kind of dirt-blond hair and piercing blue eyes. He was carrying a saw on his shoulder and I had two spare cylinders. John Paul and James carried axes and other forcible entry tools.

When we were a block from the scene, we ran into a businessman – he would have been well-dressed, if his hair wasn't all dishevelled and he wasn't covered with dust from head to toe – who was having trouble breathing. He was visibly distressed, stumbling, wiping the dust from his eyes, but we didn't have time to do more than hand him one of our paper respirators. It was more use to him than it could ever be to us, considering where we were headed. 'God bless you guys,' he coughed.

I noticed huge columns of smoke rising off several burning cars across the street from the Verizon telecommunications building, opposite the towers, and I could smell the acrid smoke from the tyres. It seemed like it was raining fire. With all of the jet fuel still burning inside the fallen towers, it seemed that everything that could burn had caught fire. A car tyre exploded, echoing off the buildings around us and breaking the eerie silence that had fallen. We ducked out of instinct, feeling the air temperature getting hotter.

Looking up at what was left of two of the tallest structures in the world – the higher once peaking at 1,380 feet – was overwhelming. I felt like I was two inches tall. The magnitude of the destruction was too much for me to take in at once. Where was our rescue operation going to start? Who did we turn to for back-up if we needed it? How many of our brothers had already perished?

Occasionally, the sun broke through all the smoke and ash and dust. Office papers still fell slowly from the sky. But what I remember most clearly is my unstable footing, constantly sliding and tripping in what felt like sand already part-transformed into crystals of glass. And the taste of soot and ash – gritty like sand, yet hard to spit out, sticking to the back of my throat. It was to linger for days or weeks. As we headed off West Street and touched the edge of the debris, it was like our rubber boots were walking into the edge of a lake, the ashes just getting deeper and deeper. Smoke burned my eyes, and nose, and throat. Dust stung my eyes too, but was difficult to wipe away with hands that were covered in the stuff.

It really did look as if we'd arrived at the scene of a nuclear explosion. I guess that's why the government and the media would come to refer to it as Ground Zero.

2

Going to Work

Except for the odd exploding tyre, it was deathly quiet. The sharp explosions punctuated the silence, and snapped me out of my reverie. It scared the shit out of me too. We had no way of knowing what we were in the middle of – whether the attack had stopped, or if more bombs would detonate. My only point of reference was the 1993 bombing of the WTC, and I was pretty spooked then, too.

Every sound bounced off the coating of white dust which now covered everything, amplified in the silence. It reminded me of walking through Central Park in winter with my wife. But all that was falling here was ashes – the ashes of everything that had burnt up when the planes hit the towers.

It was overwhelming just to think about it. Even the streets were like nothing I remembered. I used to drive past these towers at least once a week to visit my mom in Staten Island, but now I found it hard to get my bearings. I used to hate coming down here in the summer, when there were so many people and so much traffic. It was so bad that I couldn't wait to get the hell away from the area, but this was a different place now – a hell of desolation.

Several ambulances sat at the edge of where the towers' debris had fallen. They were waiting with doors open to take the injured and dead off to hospital. In a short space of time, their optimism would be betrayed – for few who hadn't already walked from the twin towers were ever coming out at all, and most paramedics could do little more than tend our stinging eyes.

Fire raged in a collapsed walkway spanning West Street that had been hit by Tower One when it fell. It was just over twenty minutes

19

after the second tower went down. The fire trucks under the walkway were also burning, and I think that got to me more than anything I'd seen. These machines are the centre of our stability when we fight a fire. They carry us, they equip us to handle the flames, they take us home. From where I stood, it was like watching some huge, great beast in its death throes. I had to look away.

From one of the World Financial Center buildings to my right, I saw a fire chief emerge. He'd obviously run there when the second tower came down, and came out now that the dust was beginning to lift. He seemed dazed, looking around at an area that was now unrecognisable.

At the corner of West and Vesey, I saw a bunch of guys running towards me from where the walkway had collapsed. They were carrying a stokes basket – a support vessel for an injured person – with what looked like a body inside it.

'John! John!' It was Frank Fee, from Rescue 1. Frank and I worked together back when I was in Brooklyn, until Frank, always a go-getter who wanted to see action, transferred over to Rescue 1 on 43rd Street, here in Manhattan. 'Come here and take this for me, I can't carry it any more.' I grabbed his handhold on the basket and watched Frank fall to his knees to catch his breath. In the basket was an Emergency Services cop. He was covered with grey dust and his eyes were halfway open. It looked like he was dead.

As the crew ran with the basket, every time someone started to slow we'd pick up a fresh man till we reached the waiting ambulances. I grabbed the side of an ambulance and rested a while, then made my way back to the corner of West and Vesey. The fire chief I'd seen earlier tried to tell me something, but I couldn't make out what he was saying. So much of those first few hours got lost in the enormity of what happened. I don't know if he was making sense, or if I was the one who was out of whack.

From where I was standing, World Trade Center Six was the first building on the block, immediately on the left of the north tower. In between the two was where the walkway emerged and crossed over West Street. Some guys were working above street level on an outdoor terrace skirting WTC Six, which was probably where my company had gone. I could just about make out a civilian looking out of a window up on the sixth floor, his head poking out through the broken glass. I didn't expect to see anyone up so high and he looked like he was totally disoriented. I had a real concern that he might end up jumping.

I looked around for a door but couldn't see anything leading into the building. The terrace had to be thirty to forty feet above the street. I saw a firefighter moving up a 35-foot ladder propped against some scaffolding, and started following him to the top.

A firefighter at the top held the ladder steady for me and once I'd got to the top, I did the same for the guy following me. As I was climbing, looking down, I could see the Ladder 5 fire truck lying abandoned with all of its compartments wide open. It looked as if other guys who turned up after the truck had been crushed had taken out the tools. Tools were fast becoming a priority. The 100-foot aerial ladder was flattened by a huge section of I-beams held together by gusset plates, the whole metal structure at least 45 feet high by 20 feet long. The truck had not stood a chance.

At the top of the scaffolding was another ladder leading from the scaffold to the railing and terrace, about fifteen feet above. The guy at the top held a ladder for me, while I in turn held the top of the ladder for the next guy making his way up from the street. Halfway up the fibreglass ladder to the terrace, I could see a fifteen-yard dumpster roaring with fire off to my right. It was close enough to the scaffold to set fire to it. Hopefully, the guys on the ground with the hoselines would deal with it, as I really didn't have time to think. The water pressure was definitely low, and I could see the guys were having problems with it. I just hoped we'd get our fair share of luck today. We needed it.

At the top of the ladder I stepped over the railing. I could see the other guys had managed to get inside Trade Center Six and had moved through the office cubicles. The man at the window was waving down to us, yelling something that no one could make out.

On an outdoor terrace where people used to sit and eat lunch, it was strange to see wooden picnic tables and benches burning. I could almost visualise people relaxing and making small talk on a nice day, even though the flames and smoke were slowly turning it all black. Raised concrete flower beds, all cracked apart, made it look like there had been an earthquake.

It seemed that my guys had arrived there just before me, and were now making their way up to the broken windows to allow us access to the office area. At the top I saw Frankie Fee climbing over the railing, looking agitated.

'John, I heard we lost like twelve units.' He leaned over and spoke in a low voice so no one else could hear. I couldn't believe what he was saying. 'When the first tower came down, there wasn't any warning. It just came down. Those guys who were working in there never had a chance.'

I couldn't take it in. Twelve units. Seventy-two guys.

'Hey Lou! They say that there's no more stairs in here, they've fallen away into the floors below us!' John Hunt's voice brought me back to the reality of the moment. I nodded to let him know I'd heard, but I was more concerned about getting some water on to the fires that threatened the terrace we were standing on. Several guys were yelling to firefighters on the street to send up the hoseline they'd already plugged in. Suddenly, without warning, a tremendous explosion rang out from down below us, reverberating through the terrace. We all stopped and stared at each other for several seconds. There was nothing we could have done if the floor had given way – but it seemed our luck was holding out, though it took twenty seconds or so to realise we were all going to live.

All this time, the smoke and ash were making the air very difficult to breathe. But the paper respirator on my face had begun to irritate me so much that I decided to take it off. I could feel the day was getting hotter as we moved into late morning, making conditions less and less comfortable. It would be a good idea to get the guy in the window down before he took matters into his own hands, and ended up landing on one of us.

At the windows, I looked into a huge office area split up into cubicles. Just a little over two hours ago, this place was a business environment – now it looked more like a scene from some war movie. My company were crawling in at the windows, stepping onto anything from garbage pails to flower pots to climb inside. I followed them. We headed down through a sea of cubicles, which every now and then divided into another row of aisles leading in a different direction. It started to become very confusing. We still had no idea whether the terrorist attack was over, and rumours had started to circulate that a third plane had been flown into the Pentagon.

As we moved through the offices, some guys started screaming at us to slow down. There was no floor at the back of the office space, just a huge gaping hole. To make matters worse, the ceilings had collapsed through what was once the stairwell. Light shone down from eight storeys above us.

I grabbed an office chair and heaved it down into the blackness, trying to find another staircase. I could see smoke drifting up from deep down but couldn't see where it was coming from. I listened for the sound of the chair hitting the bottom. Nothing. So I tossed another one into the pit. Still nothing.

We carried on a little further, but all we found were collapsed ceilings. Everything was coated with that white ash, that deathly snow. Finding no way through, we headed back to the front to find another route upwards. By this time my throat was totally caked with dust. I scanned each desk on my way out, looking for some bottled water. Luckily I found a bottle someone had left behind. As I rinsed my mouth and throat out, I spat big lumps of dirty yellow and green mucus that had accumulated in my sinuses and throat. Maybe our paper masks were only minimally effective, but removing mine was not such a smart idea.

Climbing back out the window, there had to be at least twenty of us working together now. But we still hadn't got to the guy up above. 'Hey, take another good look for another set of stairs,' I called over to John Paul. 'There's got to be more stairs!' Then I noticed we were getting some worried glances from the south side of WTC Six.

It was about fifty feet around to the south face of the terrace that once circled the entire building. Parts of it had collapsed, or were totally impassable due to debris falling from WTC One. The north wall of the first tower was about fifty yards away, just a skeleton of smoking steel frame now.

Smoke drifted towards us from fires still burning among the ruins. Three firefighters beckoned me over to a pile of debris about twenty yards away. A fellow firefighter, a lieutenant even, lay on top of the twisted steel and concrete. It's hard to describe my feelings at this point. This man had done his job, done his best to help, just like all of us were doing, right up to the point where his own life was forfeited.

'Who found him?' I guess it was a dumb question, but it was all I could think of at the time. The guy who found him told me he died with his face-piece on, as they had to cut it off him when they first found him. We moved across the rubble and inched our way down to him, crawling over the pile of metal and rock now at a height almost level with the terrace. The railing had been stripped away, and so, in essence, we were standing on top of about forty feet of steel, concrete and whatever else made up the structure of the tower.

I knelt down beside him, putting my hand out to feel for a pulse. I knew it was a waste of time but I had to make sure. No matter how bad it looks, there's always a part of you that can't let go of hope. Without hope, none of us could even function. But there was no pulse.

His left arm was held up in the protective position, as if he had been trying to cover his face when he died. Devoid of any spark of life, but unmarked and unscarred, he looked as if he was sleeping rather than dead. There was a look of peaceful repose on his face. I'm sure it's no comfort to his family, but if firefighters had a choice, then going out doing the job we love would be the way most of us died. There was a wrinkle on the plastic face-piece, indicating how he'd been caught in a lot of heat, and I guess he'd been lying there for at least a half hour before anyone found him. 'He's from Engine 1,' somebody said behind me. Somebody else mentioned a name. It sounded familiar, but I couldn't place the guy.

No one really knew how to act. At least the sense of urgency, of dire necessity, meant we could all bury our emotions. The only thing was to untangle him from the wires and steel beams folded over different parts of his body. We wanted at least to get him out of this godforsaken place. It makes little sense, but for us it was a matter of life and death to rescue our lifeless brother from where he had fallen. I had no way of visualising them, but I just hoped I'd never meet anyone who was responsible for this – in which case, I couldn't be held responsible for myself. We had no way of knowing how much worse the situation was going to get.

We put the guy in a stokes basket and carried him around to the front, where everyone else was still working. Debris continued falling from above, so we set him inside on a three-foot windowsill immediately above all the cubicles. He'd be 'safe' in there till we brought him down. Each of the men, many of whom had now seen a fallen firefighter for the first time, was mournfully quiet.

'Hey Lou, Hunt found another set of stairs!' John Paul called me from the front window. Battalion Chief Mark Ferran, a familiar face, was now on the scene, along with other chiefs and a few officers. We all assembled among the office cubicles. I saw a 'rabbit tool', and grabbed it – a small set of hydraulic teeth that spread open when you pump the handle and can crack open just about anything, including doors.

We all made for the right-hand side of the building, where we could see a lone door leading to a flight of stairs. John Paul tried to pry it open, but it only gave about a foot. It was enough for him to squeeze through, muttering about losing some weight, and a few others followed suit. If we needed to get out of there in a hurry, that door had to be wide open. Once all the guys had moved past us, one of the chiefs and I worked on it until it was off its hinges.

Unbeknown to all of us, John Hunt was already making his ascent up the stairs to rescue the trapped civilian. He had taken another stairway just fifteen feet to our left that we didn't see in our haste.

The rubble on the stairs crunched under our footsteps. It was pitch black save for a glimmer of light here and there, and being without a flashlight was a real pain in the ass. I could hear the banging of sledgehammers to force entry, and made it up to the third floor to help pry a door open with the rabbit tool. The other firefighters had gone on up to the sixth floor to find the guy I'd seen and bring him down to safety.

Things were coming under control. It helps to have good people working with you when you have to focus your attention so many different ways. As far as we knew, there could be a hell of a lot more injured people who were trapped and couldn't make it out – we didn't know, so early on, just how many had perished. A few pumps with the rabbit and I got through another door, into an office space with cubicles extending towards the front of the WTC. Another firefighter and myself started to search the entire floor area, but pockets of fire slowed us down. We found a portable extinguisher and put out enough of the fire to allow us to search a large portion of the floor. We found what seemed at the time to be the very best result we could hope for – that is, nobody at all.

Down at ground level, the two Johns had brought the guy from the sixth floor, a US Customs officer, down to the terrace. John Hunt had made his way up alone, as far as the fourth floor, got to the front windows and looked out to get his bearings. He hollered for the man to stay put until they could reach him. He looked pretty shaken by the time they got him out, and we decided to get him to an ambulance as fast as possible. The guys assisted him down the same ladder we'd used to get up to the terrace – it was the only way down, and he wasn't going to argue. It's a good feeling to know when you've truly helped someone, but it made me realise he was the only one I'd seen saved from the ruins. How many more were there trapped inside?

I suddenly realised how exhausted I was. I needed a drink of water and a short rest. We're only supposed to work in the turnout gear for fifteen to twenty minutes, max. Looking at my watch, I could see we'd been going flat out for nearly an hour. I needed to rest. I needed to last all day. There wasn't going to be any relief today, and everything was down to us.

I told the Johns I was heading down to the street. When I reached bottom, that feeling of being overwhelmed hit me all over again. There was devastation all around. In that little corner of New York City, it felt like me and a handful of other guys were all that was left after a nuclear war. I started coughing up a lot of crap, so much so that I needed to sit down for a few minutes. Then I walked out to the middle of where West and Vesey met. Underneath the walkway, the fires were still burning, and I wondered how to get on to the other side.

I walked north, looking for water, and ran into Pete Clinton from Engine 22. He was pumping water from his fire engine into a water cannon being used down in front of WTC Six. 'I think I lost my whole company,' he told me. 'They didn't get out before the collapse and I had to run for my life when the building came down. I never ran so fast in all my life.' He talked as he worked. I could see he was having trouble keeping his eyes open, due to all the dust in the air. But he continued to do his job, even after what had happened to his company. For NY firefighters are the bravest, toughest sons-of-bitches imaginable, with an unbeatable New York spirit. And Pete wasn't the only survivor I'd meet that day who had a nightmarish story to tell.

Pete told me he didn't know if the water was safe to drink, and that I should drink the water from the Department's cooler. I washed my face and tried to clean my eyes with a spray he'd set up at the side of the rig (that's what we call our vehicles), then left him standing there, looking at what was left of the towers.

I was starting to wonder if there was a more organised front, where someone was calling the shots. Without a radio, I was out of the loop as to how management were handling things. I decided I needed to get around to the other side, over to the east.

I came to the first block, heading up what I thought might be a pathway. After about fifty feet I saw that it was blocked by the stonework and rubble from Tower One. After walking on for two blocks, I saw a group of firefighters putting out the last remnants of the twenty or so car blazes ignited by the rain of fire when Tower One fell. Several wrecked cars had been blown around like the shells of toys, landing on top of one another. Iron girders had fallen from their place in the collapsing buildings, to become warped, half-melted obstacles. Concrete had been blasted into boulder shapes, like the most unnatural rock formations you'll ever see. Dark smoke rose from the bowels of the WTC, becoming increasingly black with soot particles. This was truly an alien world.

The officer in charge was having them pull the hose to the north as WTC Seven was fully covered with fire on its southern side, and probably going to collapse soon. I helped the guys pull the hose up the street, before walking back in the direction of WTC Six.

I tried to head east but was blocked off by fallen beams from Tower One, fires still burning underneath the debris. I decided to go back to WTC Six and hook up with the guys I came in with. In front of WTC Seven, I saw it had smoke and fire coming from every window. I contemplated going in to see if I could find anyone, but my better judgement told me to be cool and go find some more guys.

As I walked down Barclay Street, I ran into a battalion chief who was searching through the rubble and twisted steel wreckage of WTC One. He was standing in ankle-deep water looking like he'd lost something. He didn't seem to notice me at first, his face covered in dirt. I asked him what he was looking for. 'Bodies,' he said, without looking up at me.

I could see a woman with a cell phone, and wondered if it would be a good opportunity to call my wife. I asked to borrow her phone and she didn't hesitate for a second. But my call wouldn't go through. It would be hell trying to use a cell phone for a long while, as most of the satellite masts had been destroyed and the amount of calls being made out of New York had multiplied by a thousand.

There was also fear in the air. I overheard someone say something about terrorists with bombs strapped to themselves, walking around the financial district. At the same time I was hearing this, I saw a guy approaching in full camouflage gear, wearing a beret. I hadn't seen any other soldiers yet, and, in New York City, we're not used to troops walking the streets. I called out to him to take his hands out of his pockets and identify himself. I guess I was a little jumpy. He did neither. I stood and waited to find out what it was like to be blown to pieces.

He casually lowered his mirrored sunglasses. 'Don't worry, I'm with the good guys.' He winked and passed on by. If everything was already like a movie, it was getting more bizarre by the moment.

At the base of WTC Six, I recognised lots of friends and guys I'd worked with through the years. All around us, the fires were still burning out of control. It would be a long time before we were able to extinguish the flames. WTC Six was now burning pretty bad, and the floors we'd searched just a short while ago were fully engulfed in flame. I heard a familiar voice yelling out orders from up on the terrace, a rapid, high-pitched voice I would have known even if the whole of New York was up in flames. 'Lt. Squeaky', as we used to call him (he was now Battalion Chief Squeaky), was making his way down the ladder.

'Hey McCole! It's great to see you!' He looked genuinely happy. I guess, with all the guys we were starting to hear we'd lost, he was just pleased to see anyone he knew.

'It's great to see you too, Mike.'

'Hey, this is really messed up. We got a report that some guys are still alive, trapped somewhere in Tower One.'

'Where *is* Tower One?'

'That's a good question, nothing looks like it did down here. We're just going to have to do some searching around.'

Another battalion chief emerged from my younger days – he had also once been my lieutenant – followed by the two Johns. Jesus, it was turning into a reunion!

'John, I think you and your guys should work with Chief Reen,' Squeaky Mike told us. 'We're looking for a way into whatever's left of Tower One. We just got another report of guys trapped inside there.'

At last, some positive news – at least they were still alive. We all made our way into a loading dock underneath WTC Six, looking for a way into Tower One. We had to be really careful with the weakened structures, heading into the depths of the garage only to be blocked off by collapsed stairways and fire. Not knowing of any route under the collapsed walkway, we decided to look for another way around. We needed to go south, as Tower One was on the other side of the Vesey Street walkway.

'I can show you guys how to get on to the other side of the walkway bridge,' someone spoke up as we passed the front of the World Financial Center. We looked over to the chief, but he was engaged in conversation with one of his counterparts, so we went it alone. The firefighter took us through the front doors of the World Financial Center and up the stairs. At the top of the stairs I saw two payphones. I picked one off its cradle and was surprised to hear a dial tone. I told the guys that, no matter what, I had to call my wife. They all thought that was a great idea, and suddenly, in the middle of the wreckage known as Ground Zero, there was a line of guys waiting to phone home.

'Hello,' Tami's voice came over the phone with a touch of nervousness.

'Honey, it's me!' was all I could get out.

'Oh my God! I was so worried. I watched the towers fall over at Rosanna's store, and you were headed there, and I was so worried. Are you OK?'

'Yes, I'm fine.' Then I told her about the firefighter we found, and how messed up this whole scene was. I told her I loved her, and would be checking in periodically to keep her from worrying too much. I hung up, and John Hunt held out what was left of a bottle of spring water for me to wash out my throat.

We walked through a marbled corridor to a set of stairs. To our left was what remained of the once beautiful atrium immediately across from WTC One. It now looked like a playpen for Godzilla. The sky shone through the shattered circular glass, with smoke wafting up from the ruins beyond it. At the first-floor level, I saw footprints that made a pathway through several corridors then led off into nowhere.

We exited exactly opposite where the north tower (WTC Tower One) should have been. All around us the windows of the World Financial Center were shattered. Re-bar (short for steel reinforcing rods, used to hold poured concrete together) protruded from concrete slabs on top of I-beams that stretched the complete distance across West Street. Rubble was everywhere. It was silent but for the sound of burning fires. The enormity was something you couldn't get across on the TV screen. Beams forty feet long, two feet wide by one foot thick, were strewn all over the place. They must have weighed eight or nine tons. Everything looked grey, as if all the colour had been drained out of it. Fires burned everywhere beneath the fallen beams. We crawled over and under the beams, some of them still radiating heat. The dust made it hard to grip them, so moving about was becoming even more dangerous. I was fatigued but, by this time, past noticing how tired I felt, carried as I was by the single thought that I had to get to Tower One, find whoever was still alive and get them out – come hell or high water. And since we were already in hell, we shouldn't have much further to go.

*

As we navigated our way across the burning beams we split up, each man manoeuvring the treacherous terrain as best he could. It reminded me of when I was a kid fishing at our reservoir, skipping and sliding my way over the rocks that littered the shore. I eventually got so good I could run across them. But nobody was going to be running across this a maze of man-made boulders. To save precious time, in some spots we had to crawl under the beams and fight our way through.

Ahead I saw firemen forming a line up the hill of steel, getting ready for action. The closer I got to the middle of West Street, the higher the mangled steel rose. I had no idea of how far above the ground we were, but it seemed to be at least ten feet. I could see the burning fire apparatus under the walkway much more clearly once I was on the other side of it. I identified by sight the rigs of at least five companies I'd worked in at one time or another.

When I was almost at the other side, I saw that guys were reaching the area by coming in under the walkway from the north side. They'd apparently put out enough of the fires to create a safe passage through to this side. I was pretty spent, having crawled most of the way to my position about forty feet south of the walkway, when suddenly I saw it – the huge open crater three hundred feet across and half that wide. Filled up with tons of debris from Tower One, it was all that was left of what once was once a six-storey underground garage.

The steel was stacked up in the crater to a height thirty feet below ground and piled up on West Street thirty feet or more above, making a sixty-foot drop. Go to the sixth floor of an apartment building and look down. That's the distance. Smoke belched from fires burning underneath the steel and concrete, and whatever hadn't already been incinerated or pulverised into the ever-present dust that blew into my mouth and eyes.

Across the crater stood the remains of Tower One, a lopsided skeleton four storeys high on the left, angling up to five or six storeys on the right. It was hard to believe that just four hours earlier it had been a thriving symbol of our city and the workplace of 20,000 people.

I stood there with at least a hundred other guys. None of us really knew what to do but we knew we had to do something. By now rumour was rampant that there were guys in Tower One who were still alive. We had to get them out. So I started climbing the steel.

As I looked around me, I could see the grim determination that drove each man on to do his duty, but here and there you'd see some guy break down and start crying, hugging another firefighter. Other guys, too angry to cry, pressed on in rage, and still others, too numb to do either, were simply stone-faced and silent.

I got to the top of 'the Pile', as the crater was to become known in the weeks to follow. Some men had made it down inside the crater. Others had reached the very top of Tower One and then on over it, where they suddenly disappeared from sight. Once on top I saw that the I-beams were all connected by big steel plates, the tips of which jutted out over the crater like forsaken diving boards. Ten men could have walked out on them and jumped up and down without them moving at all. Nevertheless, someone nervously started yelling for guys to back down off the cantilevered beams for fear they might shift. That's all we needed – more guys getting hurt.

I felt useless where I was. Going down into the crater felt like a waste of time. There were already plenty of guys there, and I had made a promise to my wife that I would be careful. So, I headed back to where it was a little easier to stand. I'd been there for a few minutes when I saw a stokes basket being passed man to man, up over the cantilevered steel. What was it they were sending down? A body they'd recovered, perhaps. At first I couldn't tell what it was: the line zig-zagged every few feet and I would lose sight of the basket. Suddenly it came to me. I was expecting a body, but what I got was the first happy surprise of the day. In it was an Afro-American woman, and she appeared to be doing just fine. She had her hands clasped over her chest, with a paper respirator over her nose and mouth. She looked alert and, frankly, I was dumbfounded. I went all the way back up the line to see from just where the hell she had crawled out.

At the time I had no idea that this was 'Josephine', who had been trapped in the B staircase on the second floor. Ladder 6 and a few other firefighters had been helping her down the stairs and this was why they survived. Had they abandoned her and run for it, they might have perished. It's one of those things you really struggle to make sense of, but for me it's not a philosophical question. They did what firefighters are trained to do. They stopped to save a life.

In fact, eleven other firefighters remained inside Tower One for over three hours and survived the collapse along with Josephine. I knew about half of them. Lieutenant Mickey Kross, whom I had got to know well over the last seven years, was one.

I'd known Mickey before I came to Manhattan as a lieutenant, as we had both belonged to the same club and I'd occasionally seen him at meetings. About three weeks after 9/11, I was working at Engine 16, where Mickey was assigned. He'd been given a transcript from an interview that some London reporter had done with him. When I read it, I was saddened to find out about Lieutenant Andy Desperito of Engine 1, who had met Mickey coming down a staircase just minutes before the tower collapsed. They had both been helping Josephine, perhaps on the fifth or sixth floor. Each realised that the other looked familiar and they stopped to shake hands. And, yes, you do things like that in these situations. Probably they had forgotten that they both taught new recruits at the Fire Academy back in 1998. But I remembered because I worked with the two of them there, that's how I knew Andy. I think we were promoted together, too. He was a quiet kind of guy, but very personable.

Andy was only a floor or two above Mickey when the building came down, but that was too far. Mickey was on the fourth floor. Andy was found about two hundred yards from the stairwell. It was his body we found on the south side of WTC 6.

Frustrated, I climbed back down from the top of the steel. I couldn't get any answers, but then nobody had radios, so what else could I expect? No one could tell me from where this lady had been rescued.

The guys at the Pile were moving as if in slow motion. It was painfully tough trying to get anywhere in the rubble. As the day wore on, it began to get very hot. I made my way north for the first time, under the Vesey Street Bridge. The fires were still burning in several rigs under the bridge, but you could finally get through without any real danger of being burned.

There were a lot of guys on the scene now, and more were arriving by the minute. I walked out to where Rescue 1's rig was parked, in the southbound lane about forty feet from where the bridge had fallen. It was here that I saw Lieutenant Johnny Baldasare, a grade school pal. He walked up to me and said, 'Hi,' but seemed preoccupied. I asked him if he was all right. He said, 'I think we lost the whole truck...' He meant Ladder 9, the truck that's stationed with Engine 33, where Johnny was assigned. What can you say to something like that? All you can do is listen, and give a hug if it's needed – that's about it.

We were standing on the rear step of Rescue 1's rig. Other rescuers had riffled the contents right after the tower came down so, like Ladder 5, all of its compartments were open and most were empty. Someone came around with a bucket full of bottles of Poland spring water and Gatorade. I grabbed one as the guy went by and washed my throat out with the first gulp, so I wouldn't have to swallow all the crap that was stuck in there. Lieutenant Baldasare was quiet.

A face familiar to both of us came up. Keith O'Mara, formerly from Ladder 11, had been promoted to fire marshall a few years back and had arrived at the site before any of the towers came down. Covered in white dust, he looked like a ghost as he talked a mile a minute. He had run for his life twice that day, having witnessed the collapse of both towers. When you've seen something like that, you need to talk about it until you've found some relief. And he needed relief. He'd seen a guy cartwheeling down from the 80th floor. The man had hit a lamp-post and exploded into a red cloud, like a water balloon. There was nothing left of him. He told the story again a few minutes later, because once wasn't enough.

And then he told us how he lost his partner and good friend, Ronnie Bucca. 'Ronnie knew these buildings like the back of his hand,' Keith said. 'We were both standing over on Church Street. He said, "I'm going up," and bolted over to the building. He looked up the whole way as he ran towards the building and disappeared into some doorway in the middle of nowhere, like a secret passage. About ten minutes later the building came down. I never saw him again after that.'

In spite of all Keith had suffered that day, he was coping – or seemed to be.

I heard a voice behind me and turned to see guys scrambling around, screaming that they needed some rope. I jumped into the back of the rescue rig to look for some, but everything worth taking was gone. As Lieutenant Baldasare headed off, I shouldered my mask once more and headed back under the walkway bridge to West Street. I saw a door off to the left, around the corner. It looked promising – like it might lead somewhere.

Glancing around I saw John Hunt and John Paul not far away. I called to them about the door and they made their way over to join me. It turned out to be a subway emergency exit and it led to a staircase. I went through the door first. Initially, the ceiling was missing, the area was filled with natural light. We were forced to take our masks off temporarily as we crawled underneath some fallen beams, but the stairs were relatively uncluttered the rest of the way down. Only after we had descended four flights did I realise that the entire area was chiselled out of solid rock. We paused for a minute when we spotted light streaming down from a sidewalk grate up above. John Hunt was the only one with a flashlight and so, moving on again, we had to stick together or else run the risk of falling on our faces. We kept going down, all the way to where the trains ran. It was very quiet, kind of spooky.

I was thinking of the homeless people who live down there; it wouldn't have been out of place to meet one. We heard a noise. Down a corridor, a bunch of giant fans were blowing, so loud we couldn't hear ourselves talking. Past the fans was another door, but we didn't check it out, opting instead to go back to the tracks. Earlier a rumour had been going around that a train was stalled in the tunnel under the towers. John Paul went to check out the tracks while John Hunt and I waited. There was some damage to the tracks, he said, but that was all.

We looked around a little more but found nothing. Man, it was dark down there. Thinking to myself what a great hiding place this would be, I realised that my mind had begun to wander – and where it was going wasn't a good place to be.

We trudged back up the stairs, only to stop after two flights. We were wearing full gear and in need of a rest. As we stood there in the dead quiet, I heard something from down below – from where we had just been. I looked at the two Johns. They looked back at me. We must have been thinking the same thing: 'There's something down there, let's get the fuck out of here.'

As happened so often that day, I was snapped back to childhood, reminded of other days and other fears. I used to dread it when my mom would send me down to the basement to get something for her. I had to steel myself to go – the light switch was at the bottom of the stairs and I had to turn it off before I went back up. That meant I was all alone, in total darkness; easy prey for the monster who lived down in the basement and who might grab your leg and drag you down into his lair, to inflict on you some unthinkable horror.

At 41 years old I was braving the darkness again, but the only monsters I was worried about this time were real ones – terrorists. That's what I was thinking about; a couple of guys with Uzis waiting there to wipe out all the rescue workers. How perfect!

After two more landings, we reached the top, but my mind was still below.

It was 1.30 when we climbed the last of the subway stairs. Two 'vollies' (volunteers) from New Jersey passed us and headed down towards whatever awaited them. We were greeted with dust and smoke again as we wandered over to the front of the WFC, and then headed over to Vesey Street and West. Something was telling me to go back in, to give it one more look. WTC Seven was burning out of control and there was talk of pulling everyone out. I went back in.

Down under the walkway, I met an old chief who was a good friend of mine a number of years ago, Battalion Chief Jerry Tracy. We said our hellos just as some guys from Squad came in all excited. One of them threw me a satchel of rope. Thinking they were on to something, I went along with them. We made our way into an area that overlooked the parking garage crater, extending out over it with nothing underneath us except the layer of reinforced concrete. They were yelling down into the smoking haze to see if anyone would answer back but it was a futile effort. As we were looking around, a tremendous explosion rocked the walkway overhead. I saw fear fill the chief's face as he grabbed one of the firemen closest to him, pulling him in tight against the wall where it's safest, should something collapse. Luckily, nothing happened.

Now the bosses did start pulling everyone back from the scene. WTC Seven was unstable and was threatening to come down any minute. I decided to head out and the chief agreed. Reaching West Street, we found that a sexton had been set up on a windowsill upon the 30th floor. It showed that the building had moved two inches in the last half hour.

I dumped my mask with a bunch of others at the foot of Vesey and joined an idle army of guys, just standing or sitting around. We looked like we had just lost a big battle. All around were the feelings of despair and frustration that came from not knowing what was really going on. You could see in the faces of the men walking by that they knew their friends were dead, but nobody knew how many. A thousand guys or more had gathered here, lined up on both sides of the street. Guys from every borough of the city. Here and there I saw guys I knew. A nod is all I got from most; each man was alone with his own thoughts.

About two hundred yards away up from West Street was a Tex-Mex restaurant. A lot of guys were going in and out of it, so I headed over to see what was going on. Out in front I spotted a few guys from Engine 28 and Ladder 11. I had been assigned to Engine 28 when I left the Fire Academy back in September of 1984. I spent almost seven years there; it was a great place to work and I'd often regretted leaving.

Tommy Sullivan came up to me and said, 'The whole truck is missing. We think they were in the tower when it came down.' I asked him who was there. I knew three of the guys he named as well as the lieutenant. It was a tough thing to have to hear. Even months later, it's still difficult to come to grips with. I find it hard to believe these guys are all gone.

The other guys from the house were quiet as I said 'Hi', and shook hands all around. I told them I was going inside and that I'd see them in a while. As I entered I saw two big-screen TVs mounted high on each side of the bar. Over and over they showed the plane ploughing into the south tower, and shots of the towers falling. I watched it three times, and then I couldn't take it any more.

The local steel workers, regulars there, had opened the place up. One of them told me, 'The owner said you guys can have anything you want, drink anything you want, just don't throw the food on the floor.' So they'd cooked the food from the freezers and were serving it to us. What the hell, it was all going to go bad once the electricity was shut off anyway.

I got myself a plate and spotted the guys from Engine 28 and Ladder 11 again, seated at a table. I joined them and we ate in near silence. I thought about Ritchie Kelly, one of the senior men in Ladder 11 and one of the guys Tommy Sullivan had mentioned.

There was a row of phones behind the bar and several guys were making calls. I got on a line and called my father, who was glad to hear my voice. He told me that he had already heard from my brother Steve and that he was OK. (Steve's a cop who works in Brooklyn.) I asked him about my cousin Kevin, a fireman in the Benson Hurst section of Brooklyn. My dad said that he had spoken to my Uncle Tom, Kevin's father, and that he was OK, too.

'What about John?' I asked, referring to my sister's husband, a veteran firefighter in Brooklyn. 'I don't know,' he replied, 'but I don't think he was working.'

I told my dad a little of what I had seen and all the while he listened intently. Other guys were waiting to use the phone so I cut the call short but made sure I told him I loved him before I hung up. He said, 'I love you too, son.'

My dad and I have had our spats in the past and we always don't see eye to eye. But when something like this goes down, it dissolves all differences. I was glad I called my dad.

By this time the beer was starting to flow. Guys were cautious in the beginning, but after an hour, the taps were flowing freely and bottles were coming across the bar in quick succession. I had two beers before deciding to make my way through the building to see how things were looking on the other side of the walkway. As no one was there to stop me, I walked all the way across and out to the southern entrance of the WFC. The entire south side of WTC Seven was burning fiercely now, all 44 floors of it. I watched it intently from inside one of the lobbies that looked out across West Street. Then it happened, before I even realised. The sight materialised before the sound waves emanating from the collapsing building could convey the rumble. WTC Seven was down now as well.

As the dust cloud rose into the sky, I decided that I should get back to see what the plan was now that WTC Seven was gone. I made my way through the building once more. It was darker now, the sun lower in the sky. As I exited the building, guys were milling about all over the place. I saw Chief Keenan again, standing in the middle of the street, so I asked him what was going on. He answered, 'Form up a company, and you can go in and search.'

By this time, there weren't too many guys around that I knew. Most had gone down to West Street under the walkway bridge, to where they felt others might be buried. Seeing three young firefighters sitting on the curb looking very dejected, I asked, 'Hey! What's up with you guys?'

One remarked, 'Our officer said for us to wait here.'

'Do you want to go inside?'

'Hell, yes!' one of them replied instantly.

'There might be pretty bad things to look at in there. Are you ready to see stuff like that?'

'Hey, I was an EMS worker before this, I've seen my share of dead bodies, I'm all right to go in.'

I turned to the other two guys. One barked, 'Hey, it's our fucking job, man! We want to go in!'

I said, 'All right, you guys will come in with me.' I then told the chief what I was about to do. He gave me the OK, but warned me, 'Be careful and keep your eye on them.'

As we headed in, I told them to grab a backboard in case we found anyone. I took them all the way through the building to the spot where I had been just twenty minutes earlier. I was surprised to see that we were one of the first groups out in the steel. Someone shouted over to me, 'Everywhere you see a traffic cone, there's probably a body close by or right underneath it.' Across the field of steel beams and twisted metal, I saw cones here and there, dotting the landscape of the fallen debris. Smoke and fire issued forth from the ruins. A handline was spraying water into open flames that raged out of some deep-seated fire between I-beams.

I saw a cone about thirty feet from where we stood. I looked at the guys with me: 'Are ya ready?' They were silent, but followed me as I headed over to where the cone sat. We made our way over the steel, dragging the backboard with us. I was the first to arrive and I crouched down to look under the beams we were standing on. I didn't see anything. One of the other guys climbed under the beam and started moving the debris around. Dust flew up all over the place, blinding and suffocating us, making a near impossible job even more intolerable. But we kept at it.

We'd worked our way out in the rubble and steel about 100 feet east of the WFC. Over to the north there was a lot of excitement going on. I made my way over and saw that they had found a fire-fighter. I could see the stripes of his turnout coat. He was buried under a beam with rubble all around him and they were working to get him out. Towards the middle of West Street, I saw another cone and guys pointing down in between the beams. I headed over. As I approached I overheard one of the guys say, 'The only way we're gonna get him out of there is by cutting the beams out on either side of him.' Leaning over and looking down between the beams marked by the cone, I could again see a stripe from a turnout coat, and made out part of a mask. Then, I saw the firefighter, three beams lying across his lifeless body. He had black hair, I could see that, but I couldn't see his face.

It was the second time that day that I had come into close contact with one of my fallen brothers. I was thinking, 'This is someone's husband, some kid's daddy. They'll get the visit from some official from the department who has to tell them the bad news. Then there's the wake and the funeral and all the stuff that goes into dying these days.'

They had been right about getting this poor guy out. It was going to take a few of them to dig him out – and they'd need an oxyacetylene torch to cut through the steel beams.

The guys I had brought in called to me and I went over to see what was up. 'We've been digging and looking around here for a while now and we're not finding anything.' About the same moment, I saw a guy with a dog not too far off. 'Hey!' I called to him.

He heard me and looked up. I hollered at him, 'Hey, there was a cone over here, from when they had the dogs in here earlier. Can you give another look to see if there's anything now?'

'Sure, I'll be right there,' he said. Over he came and I saw from his arm patch that he was from out of town – probably New Jersey or Philly. When he talked to his dog, I caught a hint of an accent.

He had a big black Labrador retriever on a leash. He led the dog down to where the cone sat and climbed down in between the beams, which were hitting him about waist-high. Taking hold of the leash, he brought the dog down to him, then picked it up in both arms and placed it down in between the beams so it could have a look around.

The dog started rooting around but didn't appear too interested. 'Come on now, girl,' he goaded, 'find the baby, where's the baby?' It sounded weird, but I'd heard it before. My dad used to scent-train dogs when I was a kid. He used to say all sorts of weird things to the dogs. Even stranger, the dogs used to do what he asked.

The handler said to me, 'There might have been a spot of blood earlier, or a small piece of clothing with the scent on it. There's nothing now. I don't think there's anything here.'

'OK, thanks for your help, pal,' I said. It was all I could think of. Off he went in response to another call and another cone.

The guys I'd brought in had spotted their boss by now. When I told him that they were doing all right, he looked at me with approval. However, my three recruits decided that they wanted to team up with their own company and bailed out on me. I didn't have any objections. They thanked me for getting them in and I told them that it was my pleasure.

Another firefighter I'd known for a long time soon joined me. This was Barry Kipp, whom I had helped break in at the Fire Academy a few years back. Since then he had logged about three years on the job. And it was his father, a lieutenant in Ladder 11, who had broken me in some seventeen years earlier. What's more, his father and mine had worked together as firefighters before the elder Kipp was promoted.

The first thing I asked Barry was, 'Did you call your father to let him know you're OK?'

He was quiet. I repeated, 'Well, did you?'

He didn't answer me. I could tell he didn't want to even talk about it.

'He's probably worried to death about you. And what about your wife? Did you call her?'

Again silence.

'Look, Barry,' I was getting serious now. 'You really should call your folks to let them know you're all right.'

I guess I got through to him because he said, 'OK, all right already!' and headed off to make his calls, before coming right back to join me.

It was easy for guys to forget how much time had passed; it felt like it was either standing completely still, or rushing by at such a crazy rate that you didn't have any earthly idea what time it was. The dust that caked the watch dials didn't help, either. We dropped the subject.

By now it was starting to get dark. I hoped that it was dusk falling and not another grey cloud engulfing us. Lights were being set up for the night ahead. Out in the middle of the ruins a bunch of guys were making a concerted effort to uncover what looked like the remains of a fire truck. Barry and I crawled over to the spot and, as we got closer, I could see that it was exactly that. It was Ladder 105, which was based not far from where I used to work in Brooklyn.

The rig was scorched all over, having been totally engulfed in flames when Tower One collapsed. The guys had taken anything that could be lifted off it and cleared away a significant portion of the debris. These were the survivors of Ladder 105; a bunch of their members were missing as well. They sat solemnly around the fire truck as if in prayer. You could feel their anguish, but they needed space, so the rest of us left them alone.

A stokes basket containing a green body bag was making its way across the field of steel. The bag was full. I didn't find out if it was a firefighter. I never found out who was inside.

I made my way back to the entrance of the WFC to get a drink of water as my lips were cracked and sore. Off to my right I noticed on top of a beam something that I hadn't seen there earlier, a lumpy form under some type of cloth. As I bent down to see what it was, a voice up ahead of me shouted, 'It's an ass!'

I looked up in surprise. 'What?'

'Yeah, it's like part of a leg with the ass connected to it.'

I decided that I didn't need to confirm his anatomical description, so I left it alone. It would be off to the morgue in a while and that's their job.

Heading inside again, I ran into some guys from Ladder 35 and Engine 40. They had men missing as well; I'm not sure how many. They were heading in the same direction, so I walked along with them to hear what they'd been doing. We were upstairs in the WFC now, making our way towards the escalator that takes you down to the corridor leading back out to Vesey Street on the north side of the WFC. Just before the escalators, there was a bar. We stopped, and looked inside. It was full of guys.

As I stepped in, I heard one of them say, 'This is just what the doctor ordered!' Behind the bar was a fully stocked chest full of ice-cold beers. I was desperate for something to drink and sinking in my shoes from exhaustion, so when the beers were passed around, I took one and joined in. It had to be about 10.30 Eastern Hell Time, although it could have been midnight, it was so dark. We couldn't even make out each other's faces, but respectfully listened as each voice in turn murmured his story of the day. We weren't worried about being caught, or about what anyone would say. Nobody gave a damn. This was a wake.

After I had wet my whistle, I felt a twinge of guilt and headed back out on the job. I walked through the broken window that now served as a doorway to the front of the WFC, a buzz of activity immediately in front of me. By then it was about 10 p.m, but out here it looked like daytime, due to all the lights that had been set up. Guys with saws equipped with metal-cutting blades were whizzing through the re-bar, clearing it out of the way so they could search for survivors. Dust flew and sparks shot indiscriminately at anyone in their path as guys went down on their knees and began digging with their hands. Debris and objects were being handed back and thrown away somewhere, only be picked up again a few minute later.

Disorganised though it was, this was the beginning of what became
known as the Bucket Brigades.

I went inside and found two empty plastic garbage pails, which I
brought out to the site. I tried to set up a system so that while one
bucket was being filled, the other one was being emptied. But there
was too much confusion and chaos and yelling. Several new guys,
all of whom had just arrived at the scene, led the charge on the
digging. A few men would get down on their knees and give it hell
for twenty minutes or so, then fresh guys would jump in and replace
them. And so it went on and on, throughout the night.

Two chiefs overlooked the digging, their faces very grim. Tired of
standing around, I went down in the hole and started digging as
well. The dust was immediately in my eyes, my nose and throat. I
grabbed a hold of a long piece of cowling and with the help of
another guy began to lift it up, pulling it from between two I-beams.
As we began to free it, several other firefighters grabbed it as well,
taking it away from us and pulling it free. This allowed better access
to the area below the beam. A renewed sense of attack ensued and
more guys joined in. The minute we hit too much re-bar, the saw
was called for and the bars were cut away. Looking back, it was
amazing that no one was hurt.

We reached the sidewalk and grass under the beams, but found
nothing. I sat back on the edge of the beam and watched for a while.
The front pieces on the helmets around me bore the names of
companies from everywhere in the city. Off to my left I saw a box
of throwaway flashlights. I grabbed one and crawled over the steel
to do some searching.

I'd made it almost halfway across West Street when I saw a fire
marshal I'd known back when he was a firefighter. I knew him as
'Woody' and called him by name. He came over and shook my
hand, saying it was good to see me, as so many of us did during
the first few days when we were still finding out who was alive
and who wasn't.

We were standing up on top of a mountain of beams, looking
over at the remains of the towers. He shook his head, looking
pretty distressed. I asked him if he thought any other explosive
devices had been used in what happened here today. 'No', he

said, there had been enough jet fuel in both planes to cause the destruction we were looking at.

Leaving him, I headed over close to where the steel was higher. As far as I could tell, I was just about in the middle of West Street. The steel beams had to be 25 feet or more above grade (or level ground). Guys were emerging from between the beams here and there, covered with dust from head to toe.

The steel was piled up so high here that there were many places where someone might be found. I lowered myself down between two beams, stepping on re-bar that stuck out here and there from the concrete slabs mixed in with the steel and assorted debris. Down in this space, I was about ten feet below where I'd been standing. It was quieter down here, but I could still hear the guys working up above me. I shone my flashlight ahead, through the shattered concrete, steel and twisted wires that ran through the narrow void I was now entering. It seemed like there was another gap ahead I could get into, but it looked like a real tight fit.

I reached a small hole through two I-beams, which opened up into another space I might be able crawl through. I had to go in head first. I crawled in for about ten feet, the space narrowing all the time. Everything down here seemed naked. The beams were reddish in colour and the wires and other building materials looked new. I carried on a bit more but realised that this wasn't leading anywhere. I had to back out the same way I came in; there wasn't any way of turning around. I managed to ease myself out, squirming and wriggling my way back to where I had entered.

As soon as I reached that point all I had to do was to turn around and climb the hell out, up to the surface again. But as I turned, all of a sudden my turnout pants got stuck on a piece of re-bar. For a minute I felt like was trapped. I reached down near my right thigh and felt where I was snagged. I struggled for a moment, finally working my pants free of the bar on which they were caught.

I spent about another hour doing this before deciding to pack it in. I knew I would be returning tomorrow. I was exhausted from climbing and crawling all over the place the entire day. When I looked at how far I had to crawl once again just to get out of here, I thought to myself, Man, I really need to rest.

I got off the Pile and headed through the building, exiting on Vesey Street. The Tex-Mex restaurant was now deserted and darken. It was about 2.30 a.m., maybe a little later. I headed up West Street about two blocks. A bus was sitting there, loaded with firefighters waiting to be driven home. I asked the officer standing in front of the bus where it was headed. He said, 'The Bronx. Why, do you need a ride?'

'Yeah,'

'Where are you headed?'

I told him. He came right back with the bad news. 'Well, this bus can take you uptown but you'll have to get dropped off somewhere up near where you live and make your own way after that.'

'That's fine,' I said, just glad to have what he offered at this hour of the morning. I climbed on board and a few minutes later we set off north. As we went up West Street, I saw guys were still arriving in the quiet of the night.

The bus driver pulled over and let me out. I still had quite a walk ahead of me. Reaching the next main avenue, I managed to flag down a city bus for a ride to the cross-street that I lived on. From there all I had to do was walk for about eight long city blocks. I was in the centre of part of Harlem, which wasn't known as one of the safest areas to be walking through at 3 a.m.

Heading down the first block, I saw a bunch of guys hanging out in front of a building. Their voices were loud and I hoped there wasn't going to be a confrontation. I was almost up to them when I noticed that their attention was on me, but I just kept walking.

I was in the middle of the gang when one of them called out to me, 'Hey, Mister... are you a fireman?'

They were all quiet. 'Yes, I am,' was all I said.

The guy who asked me exclaimed, 'See, I told you! You just came back from Ground Zero, right?'

I didn't know what the fuck he was talking about, I wasn't aware of the new handle the area had been given. I said, 'I'm coming home from the World Trade Center disaster.'

That captured their attention. There had to be at least nine guys standing there and after that, the questions came at me at a blinding pace. I answered each question with respect and they shook my hand every time an answer was given.They had just polished off a big bottle of Hennessey, they told me, and so they were all feeling pretty good.

The question and answer session died out after about ten minutes and I excused myself, telling them that I really ought to be on my way. Once again, they all shook my hand and expressed to me their heartfelt sympathy and admiration. As I left them I felt really good about being received in such a way; it doesn't happen too often.

Reaching my house, I felt a sense of relief. I stripped off all of my clothes out in the hall. My turnout jacket and pants were coated with white powder. I just threw them on the floor.

My wife was waiting for me when I walked through the door. As we embraced, she said, 'I'm so glad you're finally home.' All I could think about was the wives who were sitting up, unable to sleep, waiting for some word about where their husband might be.

She followed me into the bathroom where I undressed and took a long shower. She stood there listening as I told her what had gone on that day, popping my head in and out of the shower curtain to make a point now and then.

Eventually she said she was heading to bed. There were many more stories to tell but she needed to get some sleep. As she left she said, 'Be quiet coming into the bedroom, the baby was stirring just before you came in the door.'

I finally got to bed around 3.30. My mind was a whirling series of pictures from the events of the last eighteen hours and I knew I wasn't going to sleep. But I lay in bed just the same, to rest the body for the long day ahead.

3

The Day After

I tossed and turned all night long with visions of what I'd seen the day before. I had to get up at least four times to hack up all the crap I'd ingested during the day. The stuff I coughed up had a yellowish hue to it, whereas most of what I usually spit up after a fire is black.

At some point I was able to fall asleep. I slept for maybe 45 minutes before I was woken by a nightmare I can't recall. Rolling out of bed, my knees felt chafed, reddened and bleeding from crawling around amid all the wrecked steel.

I knew there would be problems at the firehouse in getting the guys organised, so I took a little time to get myself sorted out for the long day ahead. I was scheduled for another 24-hour shift. Washing my face in the sink, I wondered how the Department was going to be reconstructed. We knew that a lot of the big chiefs had been killed the previous day. Someone was going to have to wear their shoes and make decisions that would affect the 11,000 firefighters still on the job.

I drank fruit juice straight from the container and went into the bedroom to kiss my wife goodbye. I told her I'd see her tomorrow. Once again, she made me promise to be careful.

Out in the hall, my turnout gear sat where I'd left it last night. It was covered with the white powder that had touched everything the previous day. I took it outside and shook it all out. It was another warm day, so I opted to carry my jacket and helmet for the seven or so blocks I had to walk.

I hoped maybe a gypsy cab driver would be kind enough to stop and give me a ride. We didn't get many regular cabs up around where I lived, and the thought of having to walk all the way to the firehouse with my gear on didn't thrill me. Last night a gypsy cab had stopped when I flagged him down for a ride home at 3 a.m. But when I'd told him I didn't have any money he left me flat at 118th Street and Lenox Avenue. Hell, everybody's got to make a living – I guess New York's adoration for its new 'heroes' didn't stretch to a cab fee.

I got to Third Avenue, and still no ride. A few of the locals waved to me. I could feel their care and concern and it made me feel good, but a little sad. It reminded me of how they associated me with FDNY. It reminded me of how I didn't yet know who was gone, and how many.

At the last five blocks, a city bus pulled over and the door opened. The driver, a thirty-something black woman, said, 'You look like you might need a ride.' I gratefully accepted and walked up the steps to stand next to her, holding on the railing. Passengers stared from the seats behind me as we headed down the few short blocks. None of them said anything, and neither did the driver. But what was there to say?

The firehouse was a relatively new one, built around the early sixties. It was two storeys high and sat on the corner of 124th Street and Third Avenue, a one way street going uptown. When you walked in, you were greeted by the smell of diesel oil.

In the back of the firehouse there were coat racks where firefighters hung up their gear. When it got all wet and smelly, they took it out to an enclosed alleyway and hung it up to dry. The helmets were all placed on top of the racks, adorned with buttons and little trinkets found at fires. A real beat-up looking helmet was a sign that you'd been to a good few fires. Back in the old days (eight or so years ago), our helmets were made of leather and, after a while, got that real salty 'been on the job fifteen years' look.

'The Job' had replaced our helmets with new ones over the past eight years, and a lot of guys resented it – the old ones fit better, were lighter, and looked cooler too.

Outside, guys were hosing their gear off. Inside, I promptly ran into the battalion chief, who shouted at me, 'Hey, didn't I change your group... you're not due in today?!' He was obviously upset, so

I politely told him he might have mixed me up with someone else.

I went into the kitchen and there were guys all over the place – more so than usual due to the recall procedure. The kitchen in the firehouse is where everything takes place. Everyone pitches in to help prepare meals and one guy oversees everything – he's 'the Cook'. Anyone can cook as long as they don't fuck it up. If you fuck it up, you don't get another chance. But, after working there a month, you could get a job preparing food at any restaurant – I can assure you that some of the best meals I've ever had have been at the firehouse. (Every Sunday the whole kitchen is overhauled, and the entire stove taken apart and cleaned by a junior man. When I was young, it seemed I was always hungover on Sunday morning and always had my head in the oven. I think life was trying to tell me something, but I wasn't ready to listen.)

The kitchen is also the place where all the ball-breaking goes on. It's where everyone finds out which of your buttons they can press. It can be a cruel place at times, and nothing is sacred. But if a guy can't stand up to a little ball-busting, what will he be like when the shit hits the fan at a fire? That's the reasoning behind it, and it became the measuring stick used to judge whether or not a guy was worth his salt.

I wasn't in total agreement with it, but it was fun. I grew up in a household where my kitchen at home was just an extension of the firehouse kitchen, so it didn't seem like any kind of aberration to me. In the kitchen, only the strongest survive.

We were all now on a 24 hour on/24 hour off schedule, which meant that half of the Department was working at any given time compared to about a quarter on a normal working schedule. So guys were doing anything to keep busy.

I went upstairs to the chief's office to see what kind of day was in store for us. He looked busy, hanging up the phone and telling me there would be a bus coming to take a limited number of men down to the WTC site. 'I don't know when, so don't ask me.' He seemed frustrated with the way things were being run down at the site. Two chiefs previously assigned to this firehouse were now gone missing, caught in the lobby of the Marriott Hotel when Tower Two fell. The Marriott had been located on the southwest corner of the WTC block, and when the south tower was hit some of the plane wreckage came through the hotel roof. Two companies had gone in to help evacuation, but when Tower Two came down it fell directly on the Marriott.

There were all kinds of rumours flying around as to how the manpower was being used. God help whoever was in charge, as he was not going to be anybody's friend. Generally, it takes twelve guys to man a fire engine and a fire truck, but we had twice as many guys at the station. The chief was getting the word that only five guys from each company were allowed down at the site at a time, and had to tell the company officers to break the news to their men. It all sucked.

Every one of us wanted to be down there. Right now. Just digging until our brothers were found.

There were reports coming in on the phone every now and then about people being found alive. It all turned out to be different variations of the previous day's rescue, when they found eleven guys alive inside what was left of Tower One.

I had a cup of coffee and resigned myself to the fact that we were going to wait a while before we went down to Ground Zero. For that's what they called it now – an appropriate name for an area where a bomb had detonated, even if it came in the shape of an airplane, and where a new period of America's history would come into being.

Outside the door of the kitchen it was a whirlwind of activity. The guys were cleaning out the firehouse apparatus floor. There were three bays where the three different units parked. Over on the far wall was the bay for the tower ladder. The ladder truck in this firehouse had an extendable bucket that could elevate a firefighter up to a window to rescue someone in danger. There was a water cannon in the bucket to transport to fires that could not be put out internally. The firefighter who rode the bucket was therefore putting himself into some really dangerous positions.

The next bay was for the fire engine, and the one closest to the kitchen and the office was for the chief. The chief's car had been destroyed down at the scene, and a brand new jeep was temporarily being used. With all kinds of flashing lights it looked more like an undercover cop's car than a fire chief's car. The rigs were all pulled up outside, out of the way.

About eight firemen were busy at work with squeegees and a hose, sweeping off the floor, pushing it all out into the street. There was a lot of white dust that had come into the firehouse from the guys who brought it back on their clothes. We knew there was asbestos down there. Usually, when there's any hint of asbestos, the whole operation is quarantined, decontaminated and treated as if it's been infected by some virus from outer space. There were all kinds of procedures to follow when it had been detected. But there was no handbook for what had happened yesterday, so we had to take care of ourselves.

It was mid-morning when someone came in with printed sheets of the names of missing firefighters. I got into the circle of guys where the sheets were circulating. Everyone was very quiet, each man only sighing or murmuring after seeing the name of someone he knew, possibly a dear friend. The pages were passed hand to hand, no one bothering to make eye contact with anyone else. Everyone was replaying the internal movie of the last time he saw this guy or that guy alive. What he said; what they talked about; how he was getting along in life; what his future plans were for himself or his family.

Now it was all wiped out.

It was starting to make me feel uneasy, and I realised I should stop. Something like that is a vacuum that sucks you into it. Pretty soon, it's all you think about, and your life becomes unmanageable to a greater or lesser degree. I looked through most of the pages and felt thoroughly disgusted. I got a photostat to look at later, when I was feeling a little better.

Most of the guys there were walking around looking helpless. Many had come in the previous day but hadn't been allowed to go down. They had checked into staging areas where manpower was being organised, but were never mobilised. Instead they were sent home, or back to their firehouses, where they would continue to wait. Procedure was really sketchy in the beginning, but we all had an aching desire to get down there and do what we could to help.

*

It was late afternoon when we got the call that a bus was on its way. Man, you should have seen the guys scrambling around, getting their gear ready. We were going to work. That's what we do! Everyone was revitalised and ready to go downtown – although I saw long faces on the guys who had to stay back and man the firehouse, especially one dejected young guy who had to drive the chief that night. But they would all get their turn soon enough.

The city bus drove around to all the other firehouses in our area. As each guy climbed on board, the guys who were already there would break his balls – but with good humour. When we arrived at Ladder 13 and Engine 22, they looked pretty shaken. Nine guys were missing from their house. The bus got a little quiet at that point.

The bus weaved in and out of the streets until we were making our way down West Street, the same route we had taken yesterday when we responded to the WTC disaster. When we got to West and Houston, there were literally thousands of people cheering us as we passed the security line. It was a tremendous outpouring of gratitude from the people who'd apprehensively sat and watched on their TVs at home. This was the only way some people could help, and I respected their tributes. 'Thank you,' some of them called out. 'God bless.' Someone even held a placard reading 'NY's heroes'. It gave me goosebumps, and it must have been like the victorious war heroes of yesteryear returning from battle. But we were far from victorious, and a lot of guys were uncomfortable with it. I could understand their feelings.

I got down to the site ahead of all the other guys. The smell hung heavy in the air. It was kind of electrical, mixed with the heavy odour that came from man-made material when it burned. A burning tenement gives off the smell of wood, but this was different.

It was unclear as to whether we should check into a staging area to let whoever was in charge know we were here. We weren't kept informed of how things were running down there, and I imagined that confusion still prevailed.

There was a big tent right on the corner of West and Vesey. I headed up Vesey to where the path through the buildings started, through the side doors of the World Financial Center. There was a load of guys waiting in line. A fellow I knew from Brooklyn walked by, and I grabbed his arm. 'Hey Pete, what's the story...do you have to check in somewhere before going in?'

He looked at me funny and said, 'No, just walk on in, there's got to be about two hundred vollies in there and nobody's keeping track of them.' Which is how it was for the first few days, before some semblance of order was restored.

So I headed in past all the FDNY companies that were waiting in the lobby. I made my way back through the darkened corridors, following the ever-present trail of white dusty footprints. I was struck with the view of Ground Zero, which was just as overwhelming as it had been the day before. Fires still burned out of control under mounds of twisted, partially melted steel. From the huge mound where the Trade Center once stood, now referred to as 'the Pile', a steady plume of smoke was rising. The smoke burned my eyes and nose as the wind shifted, blowing towards us.

There were groups of guys working with no real supervision at all. I climbed over to where the firefighter had been found dead under the steel. He was gone now, but you could see where they had cut through the three steel I-beams he'd been pinned under. I still had no idea who he was – just one lost brother with black hair, face down with three 30-foot beams lying across his back. He'd been wearing a mask, but you couldn't read his company number on the portion of the mask where it was usually written. It was a relief when I saw anybody I knew alive and well.

Spirits were still high, in spite of everything, but I was pretty disgusted by the whole scene. There was really no one in charge. The air quality was terrible and everything was still coated with white dust, so we were getting a mouthful every time we climbed over a mound of steel. I was hacking up some pretty awful crap, so I went and had a drink.

I made my way through the remains of the building, having walked through it about two dozen times by now. At the bar inside, I helped myself to a beer and introduced myself to some guys who'd recently retired from the Department. They weren't able to stand watching it all at home on the TV, so they came down to help. They spoke of the job, how they missed it, and how their lives had

September 11, 2001. Coming down West Street, en route to the WTC. This shot was taken immediately after WTC 2 collapsed.

WTC 6 is on the left. The ladder leaning against the blue scaffolding is the one we climbed to reach the terrace, in order to rescue the man trapped on the sixth floor.

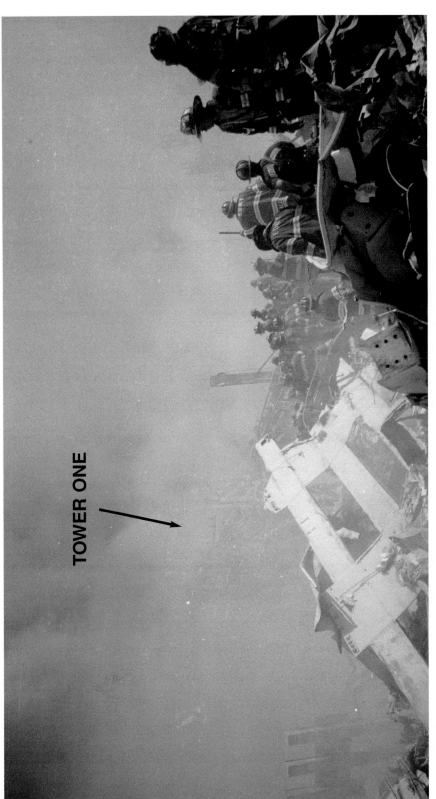

TOWER ONE →

The line of firemen were making their way towards the crater (*see following photo*). This is about where I was standing when Josephine was passed along to me.

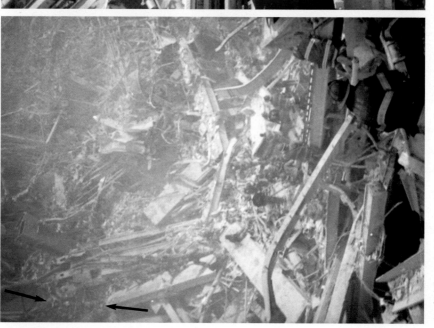

Left: View into the crater that was formed in front of WTC 1. Note the firemen in the ruins of WTC 1 (*see arrows*).
Right: Ladder 5, with all its compartments laid bare. This shot was taken at about 11.45 a.m. on September 11, when the sun managed to shine through the cloud of smoke and dust.

The view from Church Street across to West Street. The yellow, partially intact cylindrical object in the foreground was a sculpture situated in the middle of an area used for open air concerts and by people on their lunch breaks.

WTC 6, several hours into the rescue effort on September 11.

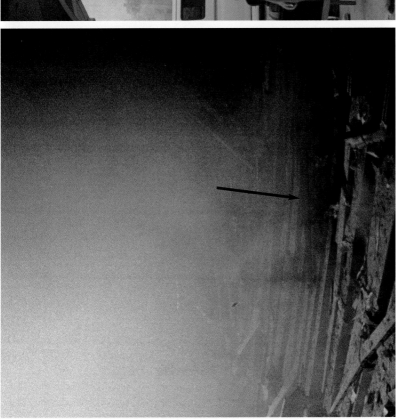

Left: This was the scene as I emerged from the front windows of the World Financial Center, opposite WTC 1, immediately after the collapse of WTC 7. Note the flames burning under the steel I-beams.

Right: A shot of me working on the special task force the week following the terrorist attack.

Following page: On West Street, the skeletal remains of WTC 1 stand next to what was left of the Marriott Hotel, right beneath the boom of a crane.

changed after leaving. Each man knew someone who was missing, and spoke very fondly of him. Everyone was good humoured, but basically broken up inside.

Close to the edge of the Pile, I met more retired guys, guys I used to work with, young guys I trained at FDNY's 'proby school'. There were out-of-town police with cadaver-sniffing dogs: if a Labrador or a German Shepherd got really excited, digging and barking, there was a good chance a dead body might be down in a hole. Sometimes the dogs went really nuts, and you would think you had something – but it would turn out to be traces of blood, or a small body part (a hand, a foot, maybe a whole limb, but only a remnant of a human being) that had been overlooked.

I made my way over to where my old company, Engine 280 and Ladder 132 from Brooklyn, was working. They had lost the whole truck company and it showed on their faces and in their eyes. I knew four out of the six guys who were missing, having worked with them for a number of years.

I dug down into some pretty deep voids with Engine 280/Ladder 132, very deep spaces where we expected to find someone. There were some places where you could actually stand up, where the height of the steel was over forty feet above grade. In other cases, we dug all the way down to street level.

Eventually I started working my way down into the crater. About twenty feet below top level, I could see voids underneath where the cantilevered steel was. But some spots couldn't be reached because of the smoke from the fires that still burned.

At bottom level I ran into an old friend from the Lower East Side, Lieutenant Patrick Rogan, and two of the guys from his company. We worked alongside each other, going so far into the crater that we eventually found the parking garage to the left of where Tower One had been. The lower levels of the garage looked untouched, the cars intact as far as we could see. It was a little precarious, but we managed to climb over a steep drop-off into one of the levels of the car park. Apparently this area had already been searched, as circular patterns on the car windows revealed someone had checked the windshields for signs of life inside. My old friend Battalion Chief Gerry Tracy climbed down into this subterranean city as well, and we moved together as a team until we came to a doorway that led to a corridor chiselled out of solid rock. It led in turn to a stairway that was all choked off with debris, making it impossible to go any further. From time to time you could hear the cranes working outside, taking down the concrete wreckage of the Vesey Street walkway, trying to open up West Street again. Sometimes we could feel the vibrations and realised the area really wasn't too safe to be searching in.

We climbed out and continued to search the deep voids further down in the Pile. At times I'd find another small hole I could fit into, which led in turn to another small crawlspace for about twenty feet, then an even smaller tight fit, then I was in a void where ten people could stand up. I was all by myself. I turned off my light and all was silent. I couldn't hear anything, except the occasional thud of the crane working the walkway. I said a prayer for all those who'd perished, and had a moment of solitude in this most solitary of places. My spirit refreshed, I found my way back out. I was getting hungry and needed something to eat.

Back at the entrance to the Pile there was a bucket of Poland spring water. I inhaled its contents after using the first mouthful to rinse my throat out. It tasted good. I was operating on pure adrenaline at this point, as, like the rest of us, I'd got little or no sleep the previous night.

I came to the edge of the Pile, like coming off of an ice-skating rink where you don't have to be so careful any more. After eating, I climbed back over to where the steel was at its highest. The entire place was lit up almost as bright as daytime, even though it was well after 9 p.m. I went down into a hole and searched around. Just as my head reached high enough for me to see out, I made eye contact with a retired guy named Ritchie Bevers I'd worked with at Ladder 132, the truck company that went missing from my old house. 'Jed!' he called to me (this being my handle when I first worked there, on account of coming in from my moonlight construction job dressed like a backwoodsman). I gave him a big hello. He'd made pretty good progress in getting a hole started and I was very impressed. It was good to see him and talk about old times.

Then it came to the guys who were missing.

It seems two of the guys from Ladder 132/Engine 280 were his neighbours, and he was a little twisted up about it. I changed the subject, telling him where the bar was so he could go get a cold one. But for now, he just wanted to dig – it made him feel better, helping to search for his brothers. Myself, I was getting thirsty again and went for another taste.

At the bar, I saw some guys from a company where I'd worked as a lieutenant a few times. There were handshakes all round and then we were silent. Nothing to say. It was dark. The electricity had been shut off sometime the previous day, so we sat in silence nursing our beers.

After two beers I trekked back out to the Pile, crawling over the steel to some virgin area that I hadn't searched yet. Steel workers cut through pieces of metal with their torches and metal-cutting blades sawed through re-bar, sending out rooster-tails of sparks twenty feet long.

It was deceptive when I stood on top of the ruined steel out in the middle of West Street, making me think I was higher up than I was. Then I got down between two I-beams and, after digging for about a minute, found they were only a foot off the ground in some places. If someone was hit with one of these beams as it slid across the street, it would just erase them, flattening them into the concrete. It was looking more and more grim as time went by.

I was outside the entrance to the WTC on Vesey Street, across from the Tex-Mex joint that was now just an abandoned storefront. There seemed to be at least a few thousand body bags. Down the street a little, I saw a bunch of guys looking down at a green body bag. I couldn't hear what they were saying, but when I looked at the tag it said, 'Possible Perp – pilot.' I found it pretty amazing that someone's body could remain so intact after crashing through a skyscraper into the middle of an inferno. But I couldn't feel any compassion, purely because of what he might have done. I heard the screams of mothers about to die, and saw the sadness in the eyes of orphaned children. It kept flashing through my mind's eye, and reduced this one dead body to something less human than those of the victims or my brother firefighters.

They were loading corpses into open trucks and taking them

down to a line of at least ten freezer trucks on West Street, several blocks away. They were big ones too, the kind you drag on a tractor trailer. I guess if we'd found all the estimated 6,000–11,000 people believed missing by Mayor Giuliani's office at that stage, we'd have needed all those trucks and more.

I walked inside, looking for a quiet place to get away from the madness for ten minutes or so. I walked up a few floors to where it was quiet and dust-free, found a quiet little nook and fell soundly asleep on a couch. This was about 1 a.m.

I awoke around 3 a.m. and managed to get my sore, aching, contracted body up off the short couch. I'd had enough, and wanted to go back to the firehouse to a real bed, where I could lie down and maybe sleep properly.

Downstairs at ground level, things were a little quieter now. Men were still streaming past me, fresh and eager to get to work, but I was spent – feeling defeated as I made my way up West Street, wondering where I might find a ride home.

Far up the street I saw two buses drop off a bunch of guys, then pull away. It wasn't looking good for me. About two blocks on, I saw a fire engine with men riding on top of the hose bed. I thought for a moment that I might get a ride, but then they pulled away. I trudged on with my head down. A few minutes later, I looked up to see the fire engine had stopped for a moment. I mustered all my strength and headed at that engine in a full run, with all my gear on.

I caught up with the rig and made my way up to the driver, who looked at me a little forlornly. He listened to my request and told me it was up to the officer in charge. I asked the officer for a ride as far north as they could take me. He couldn't say no, and told me to climb up in back with the eight or so other guys. It was crowded up there, and we fully experienced every bump for the entire ride home. 'Hi Lou!' greeted a young guy lying down right beside me. He caught me off guard. It took a second before I recognised him. 'Hey Pierce!'

It was the winter of 1998 when I first met Pierce in proby school. He'd suffered an injury while at the Fire Academy and had to go on medical leave for the remainder of the term, so he couldn't graduate.

He'd returned for the next class, however, all healed up, and had been a real trooper. I'd see him every now and then in the field, after he'd been assigned, and, as I knew what he'd been through, there was a special bond between us. Now we were sitting up in the hose bed of this rig, survivors of the worst tragedy the Department had ever seen. Our sense of brotherhood had become even stronger with all we had recently experienced.

When we finally reached the firehouse, I felt like a survivor in a war movie who'd been picked up by another company and dropped off in the middle of a foreign country. The sense of total disorientation had left me feeling out of place, and the familiar now seemed alien to me.

I knew the bunkroom would be packed, so I went into the back lounge where guys sat watching the TV in between calls. The lounge was packed as well. It was 3.30 a.m., and everyone was sound asleep except for one guy. There was a spot on one of the couches opposite where he was sitting, watching TV but not really watching it. I said, 'How's it goin'?' He didn't look too with it. 'My brother's missing...' he answered very low.

I acknowledged him but didn't say anything else. 'I'm not really too bad on the whole thing, but what's really bothering me is what am I going to tell my sister-in-law? You know... that's what's really fucking with my head.'

This was all said in a very quiet tone. All around us guys were sleeping, some snoring and shifting about. All I could do was let him know his voice was heard. We talked about what we'd both seen, and then I somehow drifted off to sleep for about an hour, before snapping awake again. It was as if I was so compelled to go back to Ground Zero that I couldn't sleep. I had to try and make some sense of the whole thing.

4

September 13/14

I spent the day off on Thursday with my wife, Tami. She felt so bad about what had happened that she got her hands on some pamphlets from our church about how to live a saner, happier life and distributed them in our neighbourhood, a veritable melting pot of nationalities and races. We were well received, and most people were happy to take a pamphlet.

Then I went to our church, where I talked with one of our counsellors about what I'd been through. She employed a system that got me to recall exactly where I'd been and what I'd done during September 11, and the period immediately afterwards – then brought me back to where I was sitting right at that very moment. It helped me to put my own actions in perspective, to take responsibility for what I'd done and to accept what I couldn't do. It also helped me to put a little of September 11 away for a while, and to get some sleep later that night.

I was surprised at how much better I felt, but it was only a temporary thing. When I got home I was all by myself. I called up an old friend who used to be a lieutenant in Ladder 11 back when I first came on the job. He asked how I was doing, and I was straight with him: I broke down and started crying. I guess I hadn't really addressed my grief properly yet. He said it would be OK and told me to hang in there. I thanked him for listening and got off the phone.

On the morning of the 14th, I was still pretty shot from the whole ordeal. My throat was irritated from the dust, and who knows what else, and things weren't getting any better. In the bathroom I had a good cough, hacking up some very noxious substances from my lungs. I showed up around 8.30 a.m. and the firehouse was buzzing: guys going home, guys coming in, on the 24 hours on/24 hours off schedule. At that rate we'd be earning a lot of overtime, but nobody really cared just yet. It wouldn't be until after the payroll codes were changed several times within the space of five days that we all knew we were getting the shaft. I never saw anything like it. But then again, our payroll department would be going crazy trying to deal with a situation for which they had no guidelines, and it wouldn't leave a good taste in anyone's mouth.

I went over to the house watch, the command station for the firehouse where all the calls come in. 'Any word?' I asked.

'No, nothing new. We went down there late in the day and it was just a lot of confusion. They were making everyone check into the staging area, but me and a bunch of the guys just went in on our own. Shit, there's got to be like two hundred vollies from all over the country down there and nobody's controlling them,' one guy said of the volunteers.

'Did they find anybody else?'

'Yeah, a few guys, but no positive IDs.'

The mood was very sombre, and I could see the wheels going round in some of the guys' heads. I made to go upstairs to see what the battalion chief had in mind for the day. Before I got a chance to walk any further I heard a familiar voice and turned to see my old battalion chief friend, Jerry Tracy. I said to him, 'Hey, what's shakin' boss?'

He looked at me rather sternly and said in a very serious tone of voice, 'You know, we really had no business doing what we did the other day.' He was referring to the search we did together back on Wednesday. 'We had no ropes, no radios, and the way they were banging those cranes around on the collapsed walkway, anything could have happened. And besides that, nobody even knew we were in there.'

I just agreed with him, he was right. 'Yeah, I guess that's true.' And I let it go at that.

Seeing the chief reminded me of the close call we had on the 11th, under the Vesey Street walkway bridge. Probably not as close as others had experienced, but nonetheless too close. The events of the day went spinning through my head as I tried to make sense of what exactly had occurred. So much had happened, so many things stuck out in my mind from that day that it became overwhelming. There seemed to be a tendency to try and just shrug it all off, forget about it like a bill you forgot to pay. But everywhere I looked there were constant reminders.

The chief and I had come to know each other well a number of years ago; we'd both worked in the same firehouse but in different companies. He'd been captain of the ladder company and I was a firefighter in the engine. We'd sit and chat about our lives together, late into the night. He had a lot of life experiences behind him and I respected what he had to offer in the way of advice, though it didn't come too often. Most times he'd just listen. There's something to be said for the power of listening. If you can just let someone tell you about something and really be there for them, they often figure out the problem themselves or come away with a deeper understanding. He was good at this.

I hadn't seen him for a few years and then, out of the blue, we'd met three times. I asked him, 'What's going on here? We keep bumping into each other.' He just smiled and said, 'God works in mysterious ways that we cannot always understand!'

I laughed. He was full of these little sayings and it had been a long time since I'd had the pleasure of hearing one. Then I asked him the loaded question, 'Any word on when we'll be going down?' There was a brief silence before he put on his serious face, 'Look, you're gonna have to be patient. Everything is messed up and the city is operating from a cope standpoint, OK?'

What could I say? I thought being an old friend would entitle me to a little more that that. But that was all there was, nobody had any solid information. There was more small talk between us and then he headed upstairs to handle the day's business.

I found my turnout gear. It was pretty trashed, and someone not-so-subtly suggested I should wash it. By this point, we knew there had been a lot of asbestos released when the towers fell, as it had been extensively used in their construction and sprayed on to the beams. The reports on the TV were very sketchy, but I believed that vested interests would ensure the whole thing was played down. I took my turnout coat to wash it off.

Inside, I saw all the stuff that had been donated by the civilian populace: flashlights, respirators, socks and other assorted essentials to keep the troops moving. I picked out a flashlight I felt might come in handy and loaded it with batteries. In the kitchen there was a whole array of donated foods. The stainless steel worktable was covered with boxes of cakes and mixed fruits in bowls. The glass doors of the refrigerators revealed the remnants of last night's meal, once again donated by our caring neighbours.

I poured myself a cup of coffee and prepared for a dose of morning conversation, or good old-fashioned ball-busting. But there wasn't any this morning. Guys were reading the newspapers for all they were worth. I wondered why. We *were* the news, after all, we all knew what was happening before it got printed. Still, I guess some guys were searching for a brief instant of solace in the media view, trying to make sense of it.

The television was on, but it went unnoticed. Most of the pictures were being filmed quite a distance from where we'd been operating, as film crews weren't allowed in there. So why bother watching? We'd all seen the real thing up close, and TV reports didn't come anywhere near to our personal perception of events – especially now, three days later.

Down there, we'd all become familiar with the smell of death. It just wafted through the air, and it was unmistakable. Being on the department for seventeen-plus years, I had the unfortunate privilege of instant familiarity with death's aura.

I finished my coffee and went out to the front of the apparatus floor, where the bosses hung out. There were three officers talking about Scheffold and Marchbanks, the two chiefs who were missing.

'Yeah, they were in the lobby of the Marriott. I think one of the plane engines went through the roof when the second tower was hit.'

'No shit!'

'You mean something actually fell through the roof of the Marriott?'

'Yeah, there were definitely companies working on the upper floors there, helping to evacuate civilians.'

'Then, when WTC Two came down, it took a huge chunk off the top of the Marriott, so those poor bastards who were working up there never really knew what hit them.'

Or so I hoped.

As for Chiefs Scheffold and Marchbanks, word had it that they had been stuck behind fallen debris, somewhere in the lobby of the Marriott Hotel; they'd been in voice contact with Lieutenant Bobby Nagel from Ladder 26, who was working with Engine 58 at the time.

Engine 58 had been one of the companies in the lobby as well when the tower collapsed. Lieutenant Bobby Nagel, their boss that morning, was off talking with the rest of the officers and chiefs when the Marriott was hit and so he was separated from the rest of the guys from Engine 58. Bobby had called to the guys from 58 that he could hear Marchbanks and Scheffold. Somehow they got a searchrope to him, they could even grab hands with him underneath the fallen debris. He had made voice contact with the two chiefs and was not too far away from them – and then the other tower had come down.

'I don't know how the rest of Engine 58 got out but it was a miracle they didn't lose more guys.'

Then it was quiet. Each man was alone with his thoughts. I sat with mine. What got me all twisted was thinking about the little kids whose daddy wasn't coming home. That's what really broke me up – that and the flashes of how horrible it must have been for all those who had got caught in the collapse.

Death came quickly in those instances, but I imagined it felt like an eternity for those who suffered it. The gravity of a cataclysm like this comes down hard and unforgiving. It knows no mercy and operates blindly in conjunction with the laws of our natural universe.

I was feeling the strain of having had no real sleep for the past three nights. I went upstairs to a lounge where a few guys were watching the tube. I mistakenly put my construction boots up on a hassock in front of me. I felt eyes burning a hole in me, and suddenly felt I'd pushed everyone back into their memories of the previous few days. I took my boots to a slop sink to rinse them off, loaded as they were with dust and debris from the site.

I sat down, hoping sleep would come my way. Somehow I dozed off for about three minutes, then suddenly awoke, not knowing where I was. After that, I was unable to sleep. The alarm tone sounded, and a few guys got up and headed down to go on a run. The rest of us were waiting for the bus to take us downtown.

I walked back to the chief's office. Chief Jerry Tracy had gone back to his regular battalion. The chief on duty looked like he could use some sleep, and didn't seem in a very talkative mood.

In the afternoon, the atmosphere began to get a little tense. Guys were on the phone to other firehouses to see who had any information on how the buses were being organised. As I stood out on the apron of the firehouse, a woman got out of a car and walked over to two firefighters, handing them a box with a cake in it. She smiled faintly, said, 'God bless you guys,' then sheepishly turned and got back in her car.

The voice alarm sounded its loud pitch and the fire dispatcher announced over the intercom, echoing off every wall in the fire-house, 'The signal, five, five, five, five has been transmitted: it is with regret that the department announces the death of the following members...' He read out three more confirmed names, and then he finished off his announcement, '...which occurred on September 11, 2001 as a result of injuries sustained while operating at Manhattan Box 55-8087. Transmitted at 0847 hours, on September 14, 2001. Signed: Thomas Von Essen, Fire Commissioner, Salvatore Cassano, acting chief of the department.'

This message was seldom heard prior to 9/11 – now we heard it every day. Previously, when one of New York's bravest (as the Department is unapologetically known) gave his life in the line of duty, he would be buried with full military honours and mourned by a large contingent of his family, his superiors in the Department, and his brother firefighters. But now our losses were overwhelming, and it was hard to know how the welter of grief and mourning that was building up would eventually subside.

Two Hispanic women made the sign of the cross as they passed the firehouse. In between the two doors where the engine and the chief's car emerged, a makeshift memorial had been constructed.

Local people had put dozens of candles and letters on a table alongside photos of Battalion Chiefs Scheffold and Marchbanks and Lieutenant Charlie Garbarini. Charlie was a man much like myself – in his late thirties, with a wife and kids, he'd been promoted about two years ago. Just like me, he was a covering lieutenant assigned to the 12th Battalion. I remembered coming in early for Charlie the previous Easter Sunday, so he could go home and watch his kids hunt for Easter eggs. It could so easily have been me instead of him, but it was poor Charlie's number that came up.

As I sat at the watch area listening to radio traffic on the Department radio, I saw the truck captain come out of the adjacent office. I stopped him and asked, 'Hey Steve, did you hear anything?'

He just shook his head frustratedly and said, 'No, I'm waiting to hear from Division.' I tried to set my mind to other things, but pictures of the 11th kept playing in my mind.

Cars slowed down out front and people stared at the firehouse. It was the beginning of rush hour and this part of the street always got jammed up. It wasn't what they intended, but the public made us feel like animals in a zoo.

The captain emerged from his office again with more enthusiasm. I caught him before he went up the stairs.

'What did you hear?' I said.

He looked at me very positively, like he'd just accomplished the impossible. He stated, 'The bus will be here in about an hour,' and then headed upstairs to tell the chief in person. The phone upstairs had been ringing incessantly, no rest for the weary. I followed up behind him into the chief's office.

The chief put the phone down and gave Captain Steve his undivided attention.

'Yes? Do you have good news, bad news or no news?'

The captain stated, 'One hour.'

'One hour what?' replied Chief O'Keefe.

'One hour before the bus arrives.'

'Oh, all right, that's good news.'

Then it was the chief's turn to speak. 'Now I have the bad news. Since we lost the bus last night and wound up being stranded we're adopting our own firm policy of assigning a bus monitor to watch the bus between drop-off and getting picked up again. So I need a volunteer to be the bus monitor, and I want a lieutenant.'

I felt a bit hot around the collar, but I knew it was the right thing to do. 'OK Chief, I'll be the bus-man just so long as you don't call me "monitor". It kinda reminds me of grade school.'

'OK, great, so McCole will be the bus monitor.' He loudly disregarded my request.

The desire to be back down there was overwhelming. I headed out to the watch, where the guys were chewing the fat.

Sure enough, the bus pulled up right on time – but the driver soon disappeared. 'Well, it's gonna be a bit longer,' the chief awkwardly admitted to me, 'that guy just went off his shift. He said another driver should be here within a half hour.'

I volunteered to tell the troops. 'Oh, this is bullshit,' one of them exclaimed, 'I'll drive the goddamned thing! Shit, I drive that fire truck out there! I can drive that bus just the same. Man, this pisses me off!'

I acknowledged his anger and assured him it would just be one more hour – but, the way things were going, I'd have been surprised if the driver showed before 10 p.m., and it was coming on to 5.30.

After a makeshift dinner of cold cuts, we were still waiting. Darkness was setting in now, and it was close to 7 p.m. All of a sudden, there was a procession of people coming up 124th Street, walking towards the firehouse. They were mostly young children, aged about seven to twelve, and mostly Hispanic, though there were whites and blacks as well. Each one held a small candle, with a paper plate cut out around its base so they wouldn't get burned by the wax. They moved quietly and formed a huge semicircle in front of the firehouse. Prompted by several older people in charge, the children started singing hymns.

I looked into their innocent eyes, and the horror of what had occurred ran back through my mind. Some of the firefighters looked a little uncomfortable. It wasn't something we were used to. The tremendous outpouring of love was overwhelming, and I got a little misty-eyed.

They sang another song and then, right on cue, the bus pulled around the corner, in front of where all the children had assembled.

The mood changed instantly, and guys went off to get their gear like a shot. It was like being woken from a sound sleep to race out to a raging fire. I thanked the adult organisers for what they'd done, and they wished God's blessings upon us.

As we left, the crowd who had just sung for us were cheering wildly. As for me, I was about to take a little ball-busting from the other guys. 'Hey Mr Bus Monitor, Billy won't stop talking!' 'I wanna sit by the window!'

I ignored it. The worst thing you can do in the firehouse is let them think they're bugging you. I'd learned this in the kitchen of my family home as much as I had in the kitchen of the firehouse.

We picked up a bunch of guys from Engine 58 and Ladder 26, who'd lost one of their lieutenants, and Engine 22/Ladder 13/Battalion 10, where I'd worked for a short while before I'd been promoted four years ago. Prior to coming to that house, I'd been working in Crown Heights, Brooklyn. I'd been getting tired of the scenery, and the neighbourhood was really depressing. I'd also just got officially divorced, and felt in need of a change of pace.

As a lieutenant, I still worked at Engine 22/Ladder 13 when covering for officers on vacation, so I knew most of the guys who'd been killed at the WTC from these two companies. Their captain was a lieutenant in the truck company back when I'd worked in Brooklyn. He was a pleasant fellow, and had the motivation to put himself through college to get his sheepskin, qualifying as a lawyer. I was told he insisted on forcing entry into every floor of the WTC on the way down, to make sure nobody was trapped on account of the hallway doors being locked altogether – some shitty security procedure. One of the guys who died with him was Tom Sabella, whom I knew very well. We'd done a couple of roofs together about ten years ago. He was a great guy too.

They all were great guys.

Companies 13 and 22 were located in the Upper East Side, a very wealthy part of the city also known as 'Yorkville'. It was the home of many affluent people, there were many luxury apartment buildings, and, in fact, it was one of the wealthiest places on the planet. I was told that their one firehouse received over six million dollars in donations – so much that they gave three million of it to the WTC fund.

A large crowd of people from the neighbourhood had gathered out in front of the firehouse, paying their respects. There were photos of all the guys who had perished on a wall of remembrance, and another memorial decorated with candles and vases of flowers. It was like a funeral parlour, minus the bodies. People stood quietly with their heads bowed in prayer; others talked in very solemn tones.

The members of 22/13 headed out of the firehouse. Mike Heffernan was one of the first. Mike's brother John was among the missing. He'd worked in Ladder 11 at my old firehouse, on the Lower East Side, only on the job for maybe three and a half years. Mike, already a hard case, didn't respond to any cheerful greetings. I'd see him running around at Ground Zero, trying to keep things moving forward in any way he could, hoping above hope that maybe his brother was still alive. I wished there was something I could say, but no words seemed sufficient.

Another fallen member's car remained right where he parked it when he came to work for the last time. Now the hood was covered with flowers, a tribute to his sacrifice. Maybe it seemed fitting, but the flowers had dried out and lay there rotting on the windshield. It was well-intentioned, but kind of morbid, and could only make you wonder about where the guy's body was.

We continued down West Street past the aircraft carrier *Intrepid*, which was docked at the Hudson River pier. We drove down 14th Street past the security checkpoint, where so many people were gathered that the soldiers were having trouble keeping them under control. They were cheering and screaming, some were crying, totally crazy with the emotion of it all. It was really something to witness. There were very attractive girls in bikini tops holding signs over their heads, reading 'We love you!' Other people were just yelling, 'USA! USA! USA!' It was pretty nutty.

We made a left and came up to Greenwich Street. A right and then two more blocks and we were there.

Everyone stepped off and the chief reminded me to be back there at 6 a.m. I acknowledged him and away they went. Before we headed off back for home, a few men, including one retired guy, asked if we could drop them off. The driver seemed to think it was OK and I was just along for the ride, so they came on board. I got into a conversation with the retired guy. He had stopped working about five years previously and was in shock at what had occurred. He told me about all the firefighters he had known that were now missing. Asking me where I'd worked, he dropped some names I knew and we joked about a few of the guys he'd mentioned.

Soon we were at his stop and he got off, giving me a hearty handshake and a God bless as he stepped down the stairs on to the street.

After a while we pulled over to the side of the firehouse. The driver shut the bus down and we both headed inside. I offered him some food or drink but he politely refused. He sat down at the kitchen table and opened a paper. I told him, 'Look, I'm going to try and get some sleep. I'll see you around 4.30.'

I'd gone a little blank thinking about the events of the previous days; the things I'd heard; the things I'd said. The time was now 10.30. I went up to watch some cartoons. Maybe I'd fall asleep.

But, in the sitting room, all the couches were full, so I went into the bunkroom. It was pitch black and I couldn't see a thing. All I heard was the steady drone of the air conditioner and someone snoring loud enough to wake the dead. One of the reasons I wanted to get promoted further was to have my own bedroom – sometimes, the bunkroom is like a barn with every kind of farm animal known to man, snoring and snorting away. I felt around for a bunk, hoping it might be empty. I put my hand down and grabbed a leg. I decided to go get a flashlight, just to be on the safe side.

As I lay down in a bunk, my eyes, still full of crap, were irritating me like mad. I scratched them and then had a small coughing attack. Soon I was dozing, but very lightly. About an hour later, the alarm bells went off and both companies were called to an accident on the highway. It had been raining gently when we returned, and now the highways were very slippery.

I was jolted out of bed, swinging my feet on to the floor with my eyes still shut, forgetting that I wasn't working in any of the companies. I was the bus monitor. I lay awake for the next hour or so, with the ongoing motion picture of September 11 playing time and again in my mind. The companies had two more runs that night before settling down to peace and quiet. Then, just as I was entering a deep sleep, someone bellowed over the intercom, 'The bus is leaving in five minutes.'

Firefighters were stirring and putting their pants and shoes on. These guys were the relief crew and had been waiting to go since yesterday morning. Each company was only allowed to send five guys down at a time, so turns had to be taken.

We made all the rounds, picking up a full complement of men to replace all those guys we'd dropped off around 9 p.m. last night. It was about 6 a.m. by the time we got down to the meeting spot where the chief had told me to bring the bus back.

I was really feeling like shit and tried to sack out for a while, but it was out of the question. I made a command decision and told the bus driver not to move or turn the bus over to anyone, no matter what. Hey, I was the bus monitor.

I headed off down the street to try to find where all the companies were. This could be a bad move, I said to myself, but I hadn't been there for over 24 hours and felt like I needed a dose.

As I walked down Cortland Street, I saw people sleeping on the sidewalk, in pitched tents, in their cars – all volunteers, no doubt. I reached West Street, where soldiers were standing guard, and headed for the World Financial Center to make my way through to where all the real work was going on. I still hadn't been to the eastern side of this mess and had no idea what it looked like.

The place was lit up as if it was daytime and there was no shortage of manpower. There was a temporary mortuary with cops standing at the entrance. I made my way through the building in the pitch darkness. I'd been through there so many times now, I could probably have done it blindfolded. Across from where WTC One had stood, there was a spray-painted sign way up high reading 'Command Post'. Facing the WFC, there was another that said 'Morgue'.

I climbed up over my first length of I-beam, my body aching. I climbed down and crawled through some twisted re-bar and then over a mountain of steel, concrete and debris. Just over forty feet from where I started, I was standing on top of the cantilever – looking out over the Pile, at the remains of Tower One.

Smoke wafted up from deep below, and there was no escaping it at times. A hoseline was running non-stop into whatever was burning down below, but didn't seem to be having any effect. Across the crater, I could see some guys moving about on top of what was left of Tower One. As the remains of the building tilted upward at an angle, only four floors appeared to remain when looking at it from West Street, on the left, while maybe seven floors appeared almost intact when viewed from the other side. But that was all that remained of one of the world's tallest buildings.

The crews inside were digging out a dead firefighter from somewhere on Staircase B2. There were others as well, so it had been reported to Chief O'Keefe over the radio. When he saw me, he snapped, 'What the hell are you doing down here? You're supposed to be with the bus!'

I told him the bus driver wasn't going anywhere. 'Well, we're not going anywhere either,' he replied, cooling a little. 'Not till we get this guy out and over to the morgue.'

I looked down the rope that had been strung up to enable men to climb down the chain of ladders that led into the crater, along the bottom, and up almost halfway to the top of what remained of WTC One. I recalled firefighters running up West Street looking for straight ladders, to get down into the crater formed when the street-parking garage caved in. We had to be about forty feet above grade, on top of the cantilever. And then it was another twenty to thirty feet below the grade that the peak of the ruins began – so it was about sixty or seventy feet down to the bottom of the crater from where we were standing.

I sat down on the gusset plate that spanned several beams. A few guys were lying around with their eyes shut. Things were very quiet. The sun was coming up and casting a golden glow on the WFC – from the east, I could see the first rays of the sun through the smoke rising from WTC One. It was very eerie, but at the same time it reminded you that you were still in the world. I decided to take out my camera and snapped off the last few shots left on the roll.

Looking east, I took a shot of WTC One, then, turning 180 degrees west, one of the atrium that was crushed when part of the tower fell right the way across the street. It had to be at least 500 feet from where I was standing, a full fifty storeys to reach that far.

The chief got a report that a stokes basket was making its way up and out of the B2 staircase. Everyone on top of the Pile suddenly came to life, descending the ladders into the crater one at a time. At the bottom of the crater we took up positions along the ladders on either side. The footing was treacherous, and it was not really possible to move very far either way, so I called for more guys to help pass the basket along.

Then I saw it and I got a chill. Could that be Billy McGinn? He was a lieutenant in Squad 18, and we'd been probies together in the same firehouse. He'd worked in Ladder 11 while I worked in Engine 28. He was a funny guy and we got along well. When I first got promoted, I kept running into him at every major conflagration in Manhattan. He always seemed to come crawling out of where the major action was, which was the life he loved.

It would be small recompense to the widow or family of whoever that was to know their loved one had been found. But, in these circumstances, it was often the best that could be hoped for.

At the start of the basket's descent, several firefighters held the rope that was tied to it. While an officer from Rescue called out orders, the men below were grimacing as they lowered the basket very slowly, inches at a time. It looked very heavy – perhaps it wasn't Billy, but a bigger guy. As the basket reached the bottom, another rope was fastened on to it and we started to pull it along the ladders.

Before it came to me, I already had the smell of death. It was pretty bad. It would transpire that it wasn't Billy in the green body bag, but another brother firefighter. Hell, it could have been any of us. I said a silent prayer for a guy whose name I didn't know.

The basket was pulled up the last stretch and on to the top of the Pile. Buckets loaded with the firefighter's personal effects were being handed down the line. There was his radio, covered with grey dust, and what was left of his mask. His company number could still be seen on the pressure-reducing assembly. I was handed another bucket, filled with the firefighter's boots and personal tools from his turnout coat. I could smell it before it arrived. I wondered how much of his skin was pulled off when removing his boots. Two final buckets followed, one with his bunker pants and one with his turnout coat. It was too much to take in, but we got through it all.

At the top of the Pile, there were a considerable number of firefighters to carry all this stuff over to the morgue. It was about 9.30 a.m. now. I made my way off the cantilevered steel.

A deputy chief yelled out at me, 'Hey! Lieutenant! Go over there with as many guys as you can and take charge of what's going on. I think they've just found a firefighter down below.' We pushed our way up to the front, got down and helped with the digging. The dog had picked up a strong odour. We could smell it too, and it looked like we were going to find someone.

I grabbed a piece of re-bar, wrestled it out of the mess and handed it to a volly. Someone came in with a metal-cutting partner saw and cut away all the exposed re-bar, making it easier to dig and clear away the rubble. Though we continued to dig, the smell was fading and it looked like we'd reached a dead end.

I stood up and looked around. We were the only firefighters in sight, even though there were 10,000 guys on the job. I borrowed a cell phone from a cop and called the firehouse.

'Engine 35, Ladder 14, Firefighter Prosaic speaking, what can I do for you?'

'This is McCole. Is Captain D'Amato there?'

'Hold on.'

'Captain D'Amato speaking.'

'Hi, Cap, this is John McCole. I'm down at the scene and there're no firefighters here at all. In fact as I stand here, I'm looking at about three hundred vollies doing all the work!'

The captain didn't get at all rattled. 'John, things will work themselves out, it's still real early and you know how the city works. Come back to the firehouse and we've got a crew to send right back down there.'

I wasn't totally satisfied, but I knew he wasn't the guy I should be yelling at.

The other guys had already headed off to find the bus. As I started out, a twinge of emotion came over me. Had I reached my breaking point? I hadn't cried much yet, and I knew it would be coming soon. As I exited the doors of the WFC, I thought of my wife and how I'd hug her and how she'd hold me as I broke down, telling me it would be all right.

And then I couldn't take it any more. Emotion came over me like water busting from a dam and I couldn't hold back the tears.

My shoulders started shaking and tears streamed down my face. I put my head down and walked north, still trying to fight off the tears till I was safely home. I looked up at all the people coming down to help.

Hundreds of people, of all races, creeds and colours, walking towards Ground Zero. Some carrying shovels, others with buckets, all united by a common purpose.

By now I was just a blubbering idiot, and I let it all out. After about a minute, the feeling diminished and I felt better. Nobody was laughing at me, or pointing their fingers, saying 'crybaby', which I guess was a fear left over from childhood.

When I got to West and Chambers, I saw some of the other guys and we all headed up to Greenwich together. I boarded a waiting bus, but didn't recognise anyone there. I jumped off and saw the guys waving to me from the bus behind. Chief O'Keefe stood smiling.

'Where's *our* bus, lad?' he said in a very accusatory tone.

'Just follow me sir, and I'll escort you to your seat.' A small cheer went up for the bus monitor as he managed to find his bus.

The ride back was quiet. Guys fell asleep in their seats. I was just thinking about getting home to see my wife. I hadn't been home much lately, and when I was it was just for sleeping.

Back at the firehouse, we washed off all the dust from our turnout coats and pants. Everywhere I looked, I was constantly reminded of what had happened over the last few days. I wished I could snap open my eyes and find it had all been just a nightmare.

I stopped at the office to say goodbye to the captain.

'Hey, you all right?' He sensed my upset, and I was thankful for that.

My dad, Sonny McCole, had been a firefighter. He'd come on the job in 1961 and spent about ten years in Greenwich Village. I always liked listening to his stories about firefighting, although he didn't talk about it often.

I can recall, as a young boy, lying in bed on a Saturday or Sunday morning, my dad coming home from work. We lived on the first floor of a big old two-family house on Staten Island, with four large rooms, a kitchen and bathroom on one floor, and a porch to the rear of the house. My younger brother, Steve, and I shared a bedroom right off the kitchen, sleeping in bunk beds – I always had the top bunk.

I'd hear my dad coming in the side door and he'd say to my mom, 'Caught a job last night, a real good one!' By 'a job', he meant a fire where he basically got his brains beaten in. All we knew was that Dad stank pretty bad. You could smell him as soon as he opened the side door. The odour permeated the house, that dank, musty, damp smell of burning tenement that I grew to know well and respect. When we'd wander into the kitchen to eat a roll and butter, he'd grab us and get the stink all over us. We'd yell for him to let go, and go running to Mommy.

I remember when I was only three years old, and President Kennedy was assassinated. I was outside with my dad, helping him to scrape the front porch so it could be painted before the winter set in. My dad had a little transistor radio, and I can recall him stopping all of a sudden to listen to what it was saying. He went rushing off inside, and I ran after him. My mom met him halfway. She'd just heard the news on the TV set in the kitchen. I watched as they embraced, my mom breaking out in tears. My father held her tight, and I wondered what was going on.

Then there was the funeral on television. I can still see my mom, Dolly, sitting on the sofa crying.

It was only three years later that a similar scenario unfolded in my household. There was a terrible fire in Manhattan in which ten fire-fighters perished, along with a battalion chief and his aide. An odour of smoke had been reported on the first floor of a building and there was a slight haze of smoke as well. A ladder company, along with an engine company and battalion chief, went inside to investigate. The engine company had a charged hoseline to hand due to the intensity of the odour.

Unbeknown to them, a fire was burning out of control directly beneath them. The floor they were standing on had been built upon so many times that it was about a foot higher than its original height. With so much additional weight (in violation of the building code), it didn't take long for the floor to give way, pitching those twelve brave men to a fiery death.

There hadn't been any way to rescue them. Half of the men were from my uncle's firehouse in the Village, not far from my dad. (My dad and uncle had a house-painting business together at the time, and it was arranged that they could have the same days off from the firehouse so they could work together.) My dad had been at home when the tragedy occurred, but as soon as he heard about it he raced off to the city to help. All I remember after that was my mom sitting on the sofa, watching another funeral on TV – a parade of coffins coming down Fifth Avenue. This time, she knew some of the men she was crying for. I was too young to know what had happened. All I knew was that I couldn't watch cartoons because the funeral was on every channel. Funny how your priorities change as you grow up.

My dad was a professional ball-buster. He was known for it at the firehouse where, strangely enough, it's always been a quality that's looked up to. And so I had the misfortune of growing up in a family kitchen not much different from the kitchen at my dad's firehouse. It was like he never turned it off. He wouldn't be happy until we were crying, or he'd hurt our feelings to the extent that we'd run to our rooms or our mother, whichever was closer or offered more solace. Nothing was sacred and he never missed a beat. As the years went on, I grew calloused by his ways. I guess I'm all the better for it – but there's got to be a better way to toughen up your kids.

My dad, along with his older sister and younger brother, spent a few years of his childhood in a care home. His dad had taken off and left him when he was three and his mom was sickly, stricken with epileptic fits. So he grew up hard, and when he was old enough he was back home with his mom and her two brothers. They were Second World War vets who were always getting drunk and beating up on each other – and on my father as well.

He could only stand this shit for so long. When he was about sixteen, he began to kick the shit out of both his uncles so that they wouldn't fuck with him any more. All of this adversity helped him become a tougher man, but his attitude didn't suit everyone. He and I certainly had our disagreements over the years.

When I was a kid, my dad always told me you needed to have a skill to survive in this world. He beat it into my head like the nuns beat the fear of God into me, at my Catholic grade school.

He taught me the importance of working, so I've never been averse to breaking my back to earn a hard day's pay. When I was in my early teens, he took me out painting with him and taught me the ropes. We would hustle through our jobs, getting the work done quickly and efficiently.

Studying at an engineering high school gave me a thorough grounding in the basics of construction. When I graduated, I went into home renovation. In the summer, I'd work with my dad on home improvements, mostly siding and aluminium trim on windows and overhangs.

I went to college for a few months, but wasn't disciplined enough to stick it out. I had a tremendous workload combined with the shittiest schedule you could ever imagine. Along with this came a lot of rudimentary problems, such as not understanding key words in various studies such as calculus, physics, chemistry, history, and even my favourite subject, English.

It all weighed very heavily on me at this point in my life, and having a few beers was always a welcome relief.

I withdrew from all my classes one day in the fall, with my mom's implicit approval. When I walked out of the bursar's office after officially quitting college, it was like a tremendous weight had lifted from my shoulders. I was liberated!

Back home, my dad wasn't too happy with my new plans. As for what my girlfriend's parents thought, I might as well have gone out and robbed a bank. They were very disapproving. But I stuck to my guns, and to this day don't regret any of the moves I've made in my life. (Well, maybe just a few.)

After I quit school, there wasn't a lot to do except look for a job. In the spring, I got a full-time job in home renovation.

It was at this point in my life that I got spoiled. I was making a lot of money, having fun doing it, and was determined to carry on doing so. I subscribed to the grand illusion of believing I'd start my own business, make the big bucks and everything would get easier – but anything in this world is usually hard-won.

My dad kept telling me, 'Take the fire department exam – it's a steady job and it'll take care of you.' My uncle said the same – a lot of folks who grew up in the forties and fifties believed having a city job was the way to go. So I went to a prep school to get ready for the written exam.

I wound up getting a 100 per cent mark. When the physical was coming up, my dad kept telling me, 'You'd better be ready for this, it's a really tough one.' He was right, but I aced that one too. It put me in the upper crust of those eligible to be hired as an NYC firefighter.

But I wasn't dealing well with life at this point, and sometimes used drugs. It caused me a lot of hardship, and some misery and pain – not to mention how it affected my mom and dad, who had given me a good upbringing.

Then, all of a sudden, I received my investigation papers from the NYC Fire Department, and new possibilities presented themselves. I straightened my life out and got through all of the investigational procedures. I was sworn in on 7/11/84 – it had a good ring to it, which I took as a sign of better things to come. I went to probationary firefighter school for six weeks, where I was taught the basics before being sent straight out into the field. The firehouse to which I was assigned was located on the Lower East Side of Manhattan, and was at one time the busiest firehouse on the job – if not on the planet.

It was a new beginning for me, and I eagerly looked forward to my life as an NYC firefighter.

But no amount of training or experience could have prepared me for 9/11.

5

The Bucket Brigades

Bryce stood in his crib, screaming, 'Mommy, Mommy, Mommy!' I was awake now, after perhaps four hours of disturbed sleep. The scenes had been playing all night in my mind. I approached the crib and Bryce promptly plopped down on the mattress, avoiding my picking him up. When I turned away he stood up again, whining for his mommy. This time I picked him up before he could sit back down. His diaper was soaked so I changed him, and fetched him a bottle.

Tami was now up and she took Bryce from me so I could get ready to go. In the bathroom I looked at myself. Man, I could use some sleep, if I could only get some. Lately the only sleeping I'd been doing was passing out after having a few drinks, something I was not used to nowadays. That had to stop. I'd have to get back on track.

After I'd washed my face and brushed my teeth, Tami asked me what time I'd be home the next day. I told her it was hard to say. Things were changing from day to day in how they were operating down at Ground Zero. I dressed and kissed her and Bryce before I left. Grabbing some extra clothes, I shot out the door.

When I arrived at the firehouse the bus was parked out front, waiting for us. The firehouse was abuzz with activity. Guys, red-eyed from being down at Ground Zero all night, were now preparing to go home for 24 hours of much-needed rest – if they could get any.

I immediately went upstairs to the battalion office to see what was going on. The chief was on the phone and very preoccupied. Motioning at the side of the building where the bus was parked, he mouthed the words, 'The bus is leaving soon.'

I nodded. The bus had arrived with no notice and the chief was now on the phone notifying all the companies he was responsible for that it would soon be by. I went back downstairs to get a quick cup of coffee before we were all chased out of the building.

I was relieved to see that Lieutenant John Rice from Engine 91 had been appointed. He asked me what was expected of him. I gave him the low-down and he realised that it was going to be a ball-busting job.

Our first stop was Engine 91 about fifteen blocks away. As we headed out Rice gave each officer three little blank riding list forms. 'These are to be filled out with all the guys who are working with you,' he told us. 'When you get to the site, the command centre is to be given a copy. I get a copy and you keep a copy.' All very well organised, at least that's how it seemed.

When we arrived at Engine 91's quarters the front door was open. The guys piled into the bus and started busting Lieutenant Rice's balls – it was refreshing to see I wasn't the only one to go through this ritual. Rice took their names, while giving back as good as he got.

The next stop was Ladder 26, Engine 58. This firehouse is known as the 'Fire Factory' and was one of the busiest firehouses in the city back when New York was burning down. They still did their fair share of work and their morale and esprit de corps was really high. Like I mentioned earlier, this is the house that Lieutenant Bobby Nagel came from.

His loss was reflected in their subdued spirits as they boarded the bus. Bobby Nagel was very well liked and a good company officer, one of the senior officers in the battalion. John Rice sat up in front taking all of the names while an endless torrent of comments was passed his way.

I asked the guys from Ladder 26 if they wanted to work with me and they agreed, so I took all their names and wrote them on my riding lists.

When we arrived at Ladder 13's quarters the mood was sullen. The bus became quiet for a while. Only one firefighter had returned from Ladder 13 on the 11th. As I've already said, I had known the captain of Ladder 13, when we worked together in Brooklyn.

It was the captain who, I'd heard, insisted on forcing open every hallway door on his way down the stairs of Tower One, concerned that people may have been trapped and waiting to get out.

The surviving firefighter from Ladder 13 had been asked by his captain to help firefighter Billy Casey from Engine 21, who was assisting an injured civilian in getting down to the street.

Billy Casey told me the whole story a few weeks after September 11, when he was giving me a lift in his car. Apparently, Billy and the firefighter from Ladder 13 had been making their way down with the injured civilian, but the firefighter's captain, Billy Burke, had insisted on searching the upper floor to ensure that no one was trapped. He was still inside, with the rest of Ladder 13, when the tower collapsed. Billy Casey and the other firefighter had only just managed to get to safety – reaching an ambulance about a block away – before being enveloped by the smoke and dust of the collapsing tower.

It was tough to hear all this, as I worked with the late captain Billy Burke ten years ago. Billy Casey was the last man to see him alive.

As we drove on, the chatter picked up and the mood became more upbeat. I sat quietly, thinking about some of the guys I'd seen on the lists of the missing. It seemed unreal that they were gone. I had heard that morning that some guys had paid a visit to one of the widows yesterday. When they'd got there a baby-sitter had been watching the kids. A small boy had answered the door and had told the guys visiting, 'My mom is out shopping and my daddy hasn't come home yet.' It broke my heart.

When we got to West Street and 14th Street, the crowds were still there waiting to cheer for us. The National Guard stood amid the barricades to keep people from coming down to the scene. A woman with a sign that said 'We love you' was screaming at the top of her lungs and as we moved through, the cheering got louder and louder. Inside the bus it was quiet. I felt undeserving of all the attention that was being given to us, and I sensed the others felt the same.

We arrived at Ground Zero and got off the bus. The sun shone on streets still coated with ash and dust. We were about three blocks from Vesey Street; all around us buses were coming and going, dropping off firefighters or picking them up. We walked past another checkpoint with more soldiers and cops who just watched us go by. Arriving at West Street and Vesey, there were a lot of guys standing around. I began to realise it was going to be a long day.

I had to check in to the command centre, a big white tent on the corner of Vesey and West Street. These were signs that organisation was beginning to improve. I told the guys to wait off to the side where I could find them, there were a lot of firefighters arriving on the scene and I didn't want to end up losing my men.

When I reached the tent, I could see a lot of guys converging on a lone lieutenant who was standing and yelling orders. Getting as close as I could, I saw a bunch of familiar faces around me. The lieutenant was basically telling us about paperwork, so I handed him his copy of the riding list and headed off. It was time for me and the guys to start working.

West Street was still impassable, so we headed up Vesey Street. We had to walk through the buildings in order to reach the other side, which is where the digging was being done on the Pile. The building was littered with trash, soda cans, and beer cans. At one time this had been a fantastic place to eat and see live entertainment – now it was a wreck.

On the 11th I had run into a guy I used to work with, at a bank of phones inside where we were both making calls. Someone had told me outside that his brother was missing and he mentioned it quietly when we met. I could see it was beginning to fuck with him; he seemed confused. All I could do was wish him luck; he was busy on the phone trying to get through to someone in his family. Now we passed each other again. It had been about five days now. I wondered how he was doing.

I looked up the escalator that led to the first floor bar. The door was open. We turned right and headed down the darkened corridor. There were signs of looting in some of the shops along our walk, but no real damage. Upstairs, the Barneys For Men store was another story. Someone had helped themselves to some of the finest men's clothing around. The store was a mess. We turned left. It was a little lighter now, then we were walking out into a big open area where a winding staircase led upstairs. All around us the windows were shrouded with dust, some of them broken. They were big floor-to-ceiling windows about three storeys high, directly across the street from where Tower One had stood. We walked across the floor and headed outside from where I could hear a lot of noise. As soon as we stepped into the open I could taste the smoke coming from a fire that still burned under the steel near us. Burning metal always gives off a weird smell and taste. And every once in a while I caught a whiff of what only could have been rotting corpses.

A crane had been set up on the corner of Liberty and West Street. It was being used to clear away the steel beams, which were now being lifted off the Pile one at a time, swung over to the side and dropped. Then they were carted off one or two at a time on long flatbed trailers. Only one crane was fully operational, but all over the site others were being brought in and set up. In some places huge wooden roads and platforms were being built on which the cranes could operate. All over the sea of steel, I could see ironworkers cutting with their oxy-acetylene torches. Fountains of sparks flew up, like a huge fireworks display. The metal workers scurried all over the steel, burning it into smaller pieces so the crane could lift them without causing too much motion on the Pile.

There were more construction workers than ever that day. I figured the ironworkers would be taking over soon enough, seeing as we weren't finding anyone alive. That steel wasn't going anywhere unless they moved it. As I looked around, I didn't see any vollies. It seemed as though they'd thinned out.

About 200 firefighters were waiting around on the sidewalk, which was now visible in places. They didn't look happy. Off to the side, the chief in charge was yelling orders to teams working close to the remains of the Marriott hotel. I saw an old friend from Brooklyn standing among them; he was also now a lieutenant. His company was waiting to go down into the Pile. I walked over to him and shook his hand.

'We've all been told to wait up here,' he said with an air of disgust. 'They're starting to pull some of the steel off and it's slowing everything down.' His tone expressed how all of us really felt. He had a faraway look in his eyes, like in his mind he really wasn't there.

Agreeing with him, I motioned my guys over to see if I could get us in on the action. When we were just standing around we felt useless. Sure, they had to get the machines to work – in the long run it made our job easier – but we felt we weren't in control of finding our friends. Tensions were running high with all concerned.

The worst thing in the world for us right now was to sit around doing nothing. Any activity would boost the men's morale, and so I went off to see whose ass I could kiss to get my men working. Finding the chief, I told him who I was. He looked at me and said, 'OK, Lieutenant, just wait up over there.'

He came across in a way that I felt was unnecessarily nasty, like I was some bad kid or something. I just said, 'Yeah, sure,' and headed up to the sidewalk where he told me to stand. One of the guys up there looked at me and said, 'He's a fucking scumbag that one, be careful of him.'

Thinking to myself, 'Shit, it's going to be a long day,' I stood looking down at the steelworkers as they lifted steel off the Pile. We were now standing at the end of Liberty Street, off to the north. The Red Cross had set up a little stand to my left where they had sandwiches and other assorted eatables. I went over to them and got a quick cup of coffee.

I met another old firefighter I used to work with. As we talked, the conversation came round to the guys Ladder 11 had lost. All he could say was, 'Ladder 11, shit, it's hard to believe . . .' before his voice trailed away. We used to work in the same area together. While I worked with Engine 28 and Ladder 11, he'd been with Engine 17 and Ladder 18. There wasn't a lot more to say. I just nodded, and put sugar in my coffee.

Down towards the Marriott, some guys from Rescue were assembling. I walked over to my guys. One of them said, 'Hey Lou, we have a pretty good idea where Nagel might be, we should go down and tell Rescue.' I thought this was an excellent idea. Maybe we'd get a chance to help out. So down I went to see what was going on.

The rescue companies wore blue jump suits, like overalls, along with their helmets. These guys were wearing harnesses as well, the ones used for rope climbing. They were probably planning to go down into the sub-basements. I could see another chief with them who looked familiar. When I got close enough I called him by his name. He saw me, recognised me and we shook hands.

'I'm working with Ladder 26 today, Chief,' I said looking around. 'It seems they have some information on where we may be able to locate Nagel as well as Chief Marchbanks and Chief Scheffold.'

He said, 'Yeah, OK. Let's go over and talk to Rescue.'

We headed over to the rescue firefighters, accompanied by the men from 26. Without being asked, one of the rescue guys volunteered aloud, 'We heard Nagel was last seen in the lobby of the Marriott. What do you guys know?'

One of the Ladder 26 guys took the lead. 'Nagel had a search rope and he was inside, searching for where Marchbanks and Scheffold were trapped. He could hear their voices and was trying to get the rope to them when the other tower came down. Luckily we were all able to get out. It's amazing that none of the rest of us were killed. After, that part of the Marriott was inaccessible, and then we didn't hear from him any more. He was right past that second column there.' Several of the others nodded in agreement.

We were all looking at the remains of the Marriott Hotel on the corner of West Street and Liberty Street. A hotel that had stood 21 storeys high was now reduced to four storeys. On top of what remained of the hotel were strewn huge beams which had fallen from the building's upper floors and possibly from the towers as well. Fires were still burning in the upper floors and a hoseline was being played over the building from the other side, though it wasn't having much effect. Beams of tremendous size were stacked precariously. It made one wonder if there would be any point in going in to search the building for survivors. But there was no question, especially for Rescue. The more danger, the more they liked it. The Rescue guys headed off to the edge of the rubble in front of the Marriott and we all stood together watching them disappear.

The other chief who had been a little short to me earlier returned. All of a sudden I heard a voice off to my right, 'Hey, Lieutenant! Get yourself and your men back up over along that sidewalk! And if I have to tell you again, I'll have the military arrest you!'

My immediate thoughts were, 'Who is this insane guy?!' My blood pressure was through the roof by now. But I remained calm, and told him, 'Chief Henry requested us to come over to share some vital information with Rescue about some missing members.'

His whole attitude changed. He knew he had been out of line, yet all he did was walk away. But he'd been there all night long and hadn't been relieved yet, so I guessed it was all right for him to blow up.

About five minutes later, a new chief took over. He ordered all units down to the edge of the steel, concrete and the remains of the Marriott. There was an endless supply of shovels, breaker bars, and gas-powered saws to cut the steel reinforcing rods that were stuck out everywhere like hairs. And five-gallon buckets were strewn all over the place – there had to be about three hundred or more.

We formed up bucket brigades in chains, back to where the buckets were dumped. As we did so, vollies emerged and joined in our efforts. There were guys from Florida, California, Ohio, you name it. You could hear all their strange accents. I appreciated what they were doing. This was bigger than anything we could be handle ourselves, all ten thousand of us.

I went up front with the guys from Ladder 26, digging among the I-beams strewn at the edge of the mess. It was like trying to dig into the side of a mountain. As we dug, we discovered all sorts of things, many unrecognisable. Shovels were useless, there was re-bar every-where. So we were down on our knees digging with our hands, filling up buckets and passing them back. Dust filled the air and I kept my respirator on for as long as it was comfortable. Saws wailed away all around me, their sound deafening. Sparks arched over everyone's head on to the backs of guys who remained oblivious as they dug with their hands, filling up bucket after bucket, handing them back along the chain. The chief yelled at one of my men to be more careful how he handled the saw. We started getting a whiff of something bad and I called for the cadaver-sniffing dog. Activity came to a halt around us.

It reminded me of being out on a fishing boat. I used to go on fishing trips where we'd be out at sea for a few days, sixty miles offshore, hauling giant codfish all day long. Occasionally some guy would get into a giant halibut and we'd all stop what we were doing to watch the battle. It was like this now as the handler put the dog on the smell. The dog didn't react at first, then he showed signs of interest. The handler told us, 'There might be something here, but he usually gets a lot more excited when he's found something.' At this point, a bunch of guys converged on where we were working, trying to help out in a spirit of brotherhood.

We kept on digging, bucket after bucket, but found nothing. Meanwhile over to our right, some guys had found a part of a leg. Like everything else it was put in five-gallon bucket, and it was carried off to the makeshift morgue that had been set up across the way.

The steel was piled up like giant pick-up sticks, larger and higher in the middle and then graduating down to street level. At its highest, I'd say the steel was forty feet above grade. Even where we were working it was about four to five feet above grade, so it was still possible we might find someone alive, perhaps trapped in a void down below. I guess that's why we worked so hard. All of us wanted to find somebody, anybody. It would have made what we were doing a lot more worthwhile.

Up above us, as the steel rose, ironworkers were cutting the huge I-beams into workable sections so they could lift them up and on to the waiting flatbed eighteen-wheelers. They made short order of the beams with their torches but the removal of the beams was very slow. As a beam was ready, we were all ordered out of harm's way. After all three hundred of us were a safe distance away, a crane would start to lift the steel. I watched as a huge steel beam was freed from the Pile – one down, only a hundred thousand more to go. And at a rate of one half hour a piece, it was going to take a long time before this place was cleared. As the steel swung out over Ground Zero, I felt weary and realised I needed to eat. I didn't have to go far to hunt out a sandwich. Seeing a volunteer from the Red Cross with a box of steak sandwiches, I eagerly took two along with a bottle of spring water.

I opened the spring water and used the first two mouthfuls to clear out my throat. I'd been wearing my respirator on and off the whole time I'd been there until it had got too uncomfortable and begun to irritate my face. Needless to say, my chest cold wasn't any better and I was hacking up a lot of yellow-green stuff. I opened up the sandwiches and wolfed them down without much thought. I was preoccupied with getting some results from all our work. There had to be a better way to remove all this debris to get down where we might find someone.

As the steel was being put safely on the truck the chief called us back to the digging. I grabbed a six-foot breaker bar and a small trenching shovel from the pile of tools and headed back up to the front. We were in a good position, getting down into some hollows between I-beams, though we were frustrated at constantly having to stop to cut out with the re-bar.

We were now getting a very strong smell. This time I called the chief over to have a whiff and he agreed. The dog was called for. All activity stopped once more, everyone's attention focused on what we were doing. Right behind us a group of vollies from California had gathered to see what might be dug up. Disturbing as it was, I could understand it. There was something about seeing a dead person for the first time that was kind of compelling. I recalled seeing my first one and how it had felt.

I had been pretty young, perhaps 25 years old. Strangely enough, we had just finished watching a movie called *Manikin*, about a store manikin that comes to life. As the credits were rolling up the screen the alarm bells rang. A truck was on fire and both companies, ladder and engine, were being called to the scene. When we arrived, we found what looked like an old moving truck, burning fiercely. As the nozzle man, it was my job to take the hose off the back of the fire engine, with the assistance of the other guys in my company. Since it was an old truck, nobody was in any rush; we took our time and found a good position to put the fire out without endangering ourselves. The hoseline was filled with water and the men from the company opened up the side doors. Flames came roaring out and I opened up the nozzle. Eventually the flames darkened and the truck company opened up the rear doors to vent the truck out. I went around to the back, and gave it all another shot, as there was still a lot of stuff smouldering.

Handing the nozzle over to another member of my company, I went to assist in emptying out the remains of the truck. It was full of wooden moving carts, each with wheels on it and about three foot square. Everything was still smoking. Another young fireman and I were up in the back of the truck, grabbing one cart at a time and handing it back to the other guys, who would take it out and hit it with the nozzle to ensure it wasn't burning any more.

After we had taken out several of these carts, the smoke was getting a bit thinner and we were almost a third of the way into the back of the truck. Ahead of me I could make out the form of what appeared to be a manikin. I took my light and got up close to the figure. Shining my light on the torso, I saw a belly button. I asked my partner, 'Hey, do manikins have belly buttons?'

He answered, 'No.'

'Then we've got a roast here,' I said. 'I'll go get the officer.'

The term 'roast' is used among firefighters to describe a person who has literally been roasted, and is now dead.

By the time the officer came around, the smoke was pretty much cleared up. He shone his light on the victim's face and I could see its grimace of pain. The skin was charred and scaly. His hands were frozen, outstretched as though he was trying to climb up over the carts. What a shitty way to go. He only had one shoe on so, which made me wonder if he had been torched by someone. Or had he just been careless with a candle, trying to keep warm?

It's hard to describe how it felt to see this kind of thing for the first time. It was different than going to a wake and seeing a body in a casket. When you come across something like this you feel drawn to look at it and afterwards it sticks in your mind. So it didn't bother me when the vollies gathered around to see what was being dug up.

The dog made it over eventually and he rooted around pretty well in the area where we'd been digging. His handler said, like before, 'You may have something here.'
The dog was pulled away and we got to digging again with our gloved hands, filling bucket after bucket. All,the while, the smell was fading and we were starting to think that maybe it was just a finger or small part that one of us had scooped up unseen. Our efforts began to dwindle as our frustration grew. We weren't getting anywhere, it seemed. It was hot out and I was getting thirsty. A beer

would have been real good, but there was no time to go inside and I no longer thought it was such a good idea. On the first few nights, when everything had been nuts, nothing had really mattered. But now things were different. I settled for spring water.

All around me, empty spring water bottles, Gatorade bottles, soda bottles were strewn about, amid all the paper facemasks and office papers and mud. A few days ago they had started sorting out the different metals that had fallen into West Street. I had watched all the activity from the seventh floor of the World Financial Center. They'd looked like a bunch of ants hard at work and all those efforts had made it a lot easier to walk around the Pile after the first week.

It was about 3.00 p.m. The chief ordered everyone back once more to allow another piece of steel to come off the top of the pile. We all begrudgingly moved away, once again forced to stop working. It was a real pain in the ass to have to keep walking back and forth over this mess. But, looking back at the first week or so, I could definitely say that doing all that heavy, dirty work kept a lot of us sane. Working like that helped to take our minds off what had happened and because of the danger involved while performing the work we couldn't afford to let our minds wander. We were forced to live right in the here and now, which might have been very therapeutic. But it hit you when you were at home alone with your thoughts, thinking over and over how it must have been for those guys on the stairs when the building came down. The thought was similar to looking at dead people: it drew you, like when you couldn't stop thinking about something really bad that might happen to you. You could get utterly lost in it, wallowing in some dark corner of your mind.

We walked back up to the front of the WFC and found some posh office chairs that had been removed from one of the trashed offices inside. I couldn't imagine what it must have been like across the street when the tower had fallen. Most of the windows in the WFC were smashed, and parts of the tower stuck out of some of them. I had taken a walk upstairs to see what it all looked like from way up high and it was something to see. I imagined what it would have looked like if someone with videotape had filmed the whole scene from up there.

So we all sat and took a break in front of the WFC, where the Red Cross had set up their stand. Around back, the volunteer ministers from the Church of Scientology had set up a similar stand, giving out a full array of cooked foods along with everything from socks to flashlights. In addition, they had set up tents in which they were administering to anybody that needed attention. They were doing what they referred to as 'assists', simple hands-on actions which helped a person to recover rapidly from immediate stress, injury or fatigue.

About six cots had been set up and they were all full whenever you walked by, so they must have been doing something good. Right in front of the volunteer ministers' set up was a triage centre to handle guys with minor injuries. After receiving attention from the medical doctors who worked there, they would be sent over to get some food and if necessary assistance from the volunteer ministers.

I grabbed a sandwich from one of the volunteers and ate it quickly. I was still meeting lots of guys I'd known over the years and it was good to see them all. I just wished it had been under better circumstances.

I watched as the steel rose from the top of the Pile, knocking over smaller pieces as it was lifted up. Below it and at a safe distance, an ironworker held a tether line which had been tied on to the steel to help guide it around. The ironworker scampered over the debris not unlike a ballet dancer; it was quite something to witness. All the while he held on to a rope attached to a huge seven-ton piece of I-beam. The beam was swung around in a semicircle and placed gently down on the flatbed.

A few minutes later, the chief gave the signal for us to resume. Some guys had already started down to the dig. This would probably be our last opportunity that day – the bus was supposed to be picking us up at 6 p.m. – so we all headed over for one last try. When we got there, we pushed our way right up to the front, among the I-beams. The guys to my immediate right were getting an odour so strong they didn't even bother calling a dog. A few minutes later, one of them found part of what looked like a leg. It was like a hunk of meat, with a big bone sticking out of it – it must have been the femur, judging from the size of it. They put it in a bucket and one of them carried it off to the morgue.

Elsewhere a dog was searching amid lots of excitement. We kept digging, looking, but we weren't finding anything. Over on the right, it was confirmed that they'd found a body. A firefighter? That was what everybody was thinking. Immediately I started to think again about Charlie Garbarini. We had come to know each other over the last year or so. As we were both covering officers, we had had few opportunities to work with one another, but it did occasionally happen. On those occasions we had had a lot of laughs together; he had a wonderful sense of humour. Now he was missing, but it could have been me. I could have been working in the company where he'd been working that day. I guessed it just wasn't my turn.

More news came over from where they'd found the body. It wasn't a fireman, it was a woman. We dug for about another 45 minutes, all the time getting a little slower in our work. Then, feeling curious, I decided to go over and take a look at what they'd found. But when I got there, they'd already put the victim in a green body bag and there wasn't much to see. All you could see was where the body had been and how they'd dug out a space under the beam where she'd been lying. I imagined the moment of death for that poor soul. I hoped it was quick. It would be terrible to be hit with an I-beam and then suffocate to death under a ton of debris, unable to move.

My guys were all getting ready to call it a day. We had a long walk back to the bus and I just hoped it was on time. Gathering behind the WFC, we got a little something to eat and drink. Then the guys said they wanted to try and get some of the work boots that were being given away as they would be better for working in than our firefighting boots. I agreed. I'd been wearing my construction boots since the third day.

They were a lot lighter and I could climb a lot easier on the steel with them. They headed over to where the boots were being given out and I told them I'd meet them outside on Vesey. I made my way through the WFC, once more looking with sadness at the devastation inside the atrium. It was going to take a long time before this ever looked good again.

As I walked, my thoughts were of that day's events. The chief who had yelled at me – that kind of stuck out for some reason. All the digging, the body parts found, that poor woman, the steel beams swinging in the air, the dust we were breathing in. Jesus, it was like a movie playing over and over. I wished I could switch it off long enough for some rest. I waited at the corner of Vesey for the guys to arrive. The walkway was still being dismantled still, to clear the road, so vehicles could get through.

New crews made their way past me, not paying me any mind. When my guys caught up with me we made our way to where the bus was supposed to be. We were running a little late; I hoped they would wait for us. Turning left on to West Street, we walked up to Chambers Street. The police and soldiers were thicker than ever; they were checking IDs and turning people away, some of them were volunteers. Probably, later on, when things were quieter, they'd let some of these volunteers in to help.

It was a long walk up to Broadway where the bus was parked. I wished someone would come over and offer to drive us. At Church Street the Army Corps of Engineers had begun to erect a chain link fence around the entire perimeter of the affected area. Portable bathrooms were being unloaded and set up. Volunteers from all over the USA, who had converged on the scene and had no place to stay, were still camped out on the kerbs. I wondered how much longer they'd be allowed to stay. There was no such thing as squatters' rights around there and the security noose was starting to tighten.

We finally reached Broadway and Chambers, and still no bus in sight. I got a sinking feeling in my stomach: 'Not again,' I thought to myself. The guys started walking downtown and I followed. One of them called out, 'Hey Lou! There's our bus up ahead.' He stopped and looked again, 'Well, it looks like our bus. It's a bus, that I know for sure.'

The guys laughed at him and made a few wisecracks. We arrived at the bus and thankfully it was ours. As we boarded, the razzing started and our balls were busted soundly for being late. Luckily we weren't the last to arrive. Some guys from Engine 37 were still missing.

Lieutenant Rice had made it through the day. After a successful day as 'bus monitor' he looked a little shot but he promised to stop at the first bodega and get us a few cases of beer.

After we'd waited about five minutes, a fireman came up and told us that the guys from Engine 37 were getting a ride and not to wait for them any more. Rice told the driver to head off. We were going home.

*

It was quiet as we rode along. I looked around. Over the last few days we had all been through a lot. I remembered seeing guys meeting and embracing in the early hours down on the Pile, crying openly, hugging one another, glad to see each other alive. It was a very emotional time for all of us. Even though we were all headed for home, 343 of us would never see home again.

We made our stops along the way, everyone saying goodbye as they stepped down from the bus. Before long, we arrived in front of Engine 35 and Ladder 14. We all piled off, making our way into the firehouse, where a fresh crew was waiting to go. The bus driver asked if a few of us could help him back up over on the left side of the firehouse. His shift was up now, and I hoped the other crew wouldn't have to wait long.

Before we headed in, some firefighter was yelling at us to please take our gear off outside and wash it or leave it out there. We obliged him and stripped off our bunker gear. Someone had a hose and we took turns rinsing the filth off our jackets and pants.

I walked into the firehouse in my socks, leaving my soaking wet gear out in the front of the firehouse. Finding an empty seat in the backroom lounge, I flopped down into it.

I sat there thinking. And just when I thought I would fall asleep the pictures started again...

6

The World Trade Center Task Force

On Tuesday September 18 I dragged my ass out of bed to get ready for the new task force. We had to meet at a parking lot in Queens near Shea Stadium. None of us had any real idea of how this thing was being organised, but any type of organisation would be a relief. I hopped into my Toyota, and arrived there pretty quickly. When I pulled into the parking lot it was still dark, but there were a lot of cars and pick-up trucks all looking for a parking spot not too far down from where we were assembling.

I had to park all the way down at the end of the lot. I saw many familiar faces that appeared to be in another world, a dream world I'd left behind in bed. It was really early still. I was reminded of the times I used to go fishing at Sheepshead Bay in Brooklyn, getting up in the middle of the night to get down to the boat before she left. There was even a smell of the ocean in the air, as the parking lot overlooked a bay.

There were about ten buses lined up with darkened windows, sitting idle with no drivers in them. I walked up to a desk where I knew the officer running the admin. It was Ritchie LaFata, my lieutenant back when I worked in Brooklyn. Now he was a captain, having just been promoted a few days before.

'Fill these out when you get yourself a company, John. When you get to the site, they'll collect them at the command post.'

As I was signing in, I saw guys walking by me dressed in the Carhartt coveralls, with suspenders, that we used to wear when I was working in construction. They were getting everything they needed from a 150-foot row of eight-foot-wide boxes: gloves, hardhats, boots, coveralls, lights, masks, spray-paint. I picked out some coveralls and a light, and headed back to my car to offload my firefighting gear, which was considerably heavier than what was on offer.

This city had changed for good. But, even though there had been several thousand people killed, for us things had to carry on. Firefighters weren't expected to need time to 'get over it'. As before, emotions were welling up under the surface but the momentum of events insisted we suppress them.

I saw a lot of the guys from my battalion and from the Harlem companies, where I preferred to work. I'd worked in Engine 37 plenty of times, and had grown to like the guys that worked there – even though I'd thought the assignment desk were fucking with me at first by sending me to a particularly troubled firehouse. They had recently endured their share of personal hardships and tragedies, and a dark cloud had settled over the place. But it reminded me very much of where I'd been broken in, down on the Lower East Side of Manhattan, and after a few days I started to fit in. A good firehouse more or less runs itself, and the boss doesn't need to tell anyone what to do, which comes from years of the senior men breaking in the new guys right from the start. So when Drew Kane, from Engine 37/Ladder 40, gave me the big hello, I told him I needed to get a company together. He agreed, so we got all kinds of stuff from the boxes, including spray-paint for marking searched voids. A short while later, I had a full complement of firefighters from Engine 37 to put on my riding list.

The Liberty Street command post was located almost in front of Engine 10 and Ladder 10, which were right across from the south tower. Being so close, these two companies were the first expected, or 'first due' companies to respond to the WTC scene. I don't know what time they arrived, but they did suffer some losses.

Liberty Street used to be a thriving area at all times. Now, several of its restaurants had been converted into tool depots, and food suppliers for the rescuers. Some had been totally trashed, and looked like they had been looted. Scattered food containers lay all about the floor, their shelves emptied of anything that could be used.

There was already an engine company waiting to be relieved. As it turned out, we were already one hour late. We apologised to those guys, not knowing that all we were going to do was sit on a two-and-a-half inch handline (this is a rather unwieldy hose).

The handline that we were in charge of was a back-up, should the main one become unserviceable. The main handline was being used on some smouldering fires burning deep below the surface of the Pile. It didn't bode well for the day.

I hadn't been over to this side of the Pile yet, and it was overwhelming to witness it. The steel from the collapsed WTC Two had to be thirty to forty feet high in some places, and it was getting harder to believe, or to hope, that there was anyone alive under all that. Yet hope was all we had, even though seemingly unstoppable flames continued to burn deep below the surface.

Dump trucks were moving into position to receive bucketfuls of debris that had been sifted by firefighting crews. There was a long trailer serving as the command centre. I went to see the chiefs, but didn't recognise anyone. I soon realised they'd all been captains just a few days ago, and had attained their new rank on the last day marked for mass promotion, Sunday the 16th. The chiefs were doing their best, and I didn't envy them for a moment. There was only so much any one man could do in view of the magnitude of what had happened.

The chief in charge turned out to be the son of my deputy chief when I'd been a young firefighter. He warned me it was going to be a real low-key day, and to make sure we kept an eye on the handline. Any illusions that we were going to be assisting in the search were shattered when we saw teams of FEMA guys – Federal Emergency Management Agency – arriving by the dozen. It was killing our men to be sitting around, watching everyone else do all the work. Things got so boring that they resorted to sweeping the street, cleaning up all the debris that had accumulated. It was far from glamorous, but it gave them a sense of satisfaction. No one was going to tell them to stop, not while I was their boss.

Immediately behind us, I could see how the Bankers' Trust building had been raked by the falling of Tower Two. Floors of offices were exposed to the open air, Venetian blinds swinging in the breeze, and most windows were shattered or missing on the façade. Some continued to fall out, as a result of the building gradually shifting in its foundations. Construction crews were busily setting up netting from the top of the building down to protect everyone from the falling glass.

All of a sudden, I saw something out of the corner of my eye as a bulldozer picked up some debris from the street. It looked like part of the reflective tape from a firefighter's turnout coat. I yelled over the din of the heavy machinery, telling the driver to stop. He looked the other way in disgust, and stopped scooping. I ignored him and hurriedly checked through the debris.

I was mistaken.

'Hey Lou, you see something?' one of our guys said.

'I thought I saw a piece of turnout coat, but it was just a piece of plastic.'

'Those guys give you a hard time?'

'No, not really, but it just seems like they don't really give a fuck. They're treating this whole thing like it's just one big construction site.' I looked back at the bulldozer, now moving away from us.

The men were quiet now. Rumours were coming in to us that there were all kinds of bucket brigades being organised at the West Street command centre. That would be better than what we were doing, for sure. In fact, anything would be better. My men were sitting in chairs underneath a canopy. There were tables as well, and it looked like a cafe except there was no waitress. They smoked cigarettes, drank spring water, and waited for something to do.

One retired firefighter, working as a volunteer, asked me where he could find a Hurst tool. A Hurst tool is often referred to as the 'jaws of life' – it's not unlike a mechanical bird's beak, but about three feet long. It'll spread open just about anything, provided you have a good bite on whatever it is you're trying to open. We had a virtual hardware store down there that was like heaven to a construction worker: saws, gas, lights, handtools for digging, hammers, and every other kind of handtool known to man. This guy told me he needed a Hurst tool because he and some other guys believed they'd found some dead firefighters buried underneath a crushed car.

I was amazed. Wasn't anyone coordinating everything down there? Didn't anyone know what the hell was going on? But then I took a reality check, and looked around at the size of the operation. It was a wonder that, after September 11, anything could be organised at all. One of my guys, who'd been listening to the conversation, was looking at me as if we should get involved. I didn't even get into it with him. Who was going to watch the hoseline? It might have been stupid, it might have seemed unfair, but it was our job and we couldn't abandon it. If everyone started doing that, you'd have had a zoo down there.

The FEMA men looked like they were ready to go down into the bowels of the earth, equipped with lights on their helmets, rappelling harnesses and ropes. I asked one guy, who'd come all the way from Louisiana, how he came to join the FEMA.

'We-ell, ya know, they got these tunnels underground down where we come from and we all just go down in there, just crawl round down there, can't see shit the whole damn time. Do a few rescue missions and such, and dependin' how well y'all do, sooner or later you git your cert. Then, when the shit hits the fan, you git a call and you're mobilised. As soon as you're mobilised, you're gettin' paid for every minute.'

'Wow,' was all I could muster. I was beginning to get a little pissed off about being excluded from the rescue activities.

But, in fairness, I didn't think the money really meant anything to those guys. They'd come from all over the country, and they would have done it for free. We had a similar thing in the NYC Fire Department: DART (the Disaster Assist Rescue Team). When there was any type of international natural catastrophe, like a tornado or earthquake, they were mobilised. But they didn't get time off to do it, although they still got paid while they were over in some foreign country helping to save lives. The time they spent away from work was deducted from their vacation hours, so they were giving up their own time.

The day was dragging, but we were there for the duration. I grabbed a sandwich from one of the food distribution points, then, all of a sudden, saw my guys getting up to grab the hoseline. Another company was attempting to pick it up and move it, but you never, ever, give up your hoseline. It was a matter of company pride ingrained in you by the senior men. This is the type of thing that binds men together, in their relationship with the red devil, fire.

But it was the FEMA guys who were in control, their honeydew southern accents directing their crews in disassembling their set-up.

Their trailer was like a big GI-Joe toy, with things that flipped out and folded this way and that, and antennas that shot up in the air. It was a marvel to see. Now they were taking it down to move it to a more strategic position, yelling at everyone to get the hell out the way, 'unless y'all want to get picked up with a shovel.'

'Are these guys for real?' one of my men said.

'These federal folks, they have a special way of doing things. You just have to be able to understand it,' I said, knowingly.

'Do you understand it, Lou?'

'Hell no, I'm a lieutenant in the FDNY... of course I don't understand it,' I deadpanned.

I went to take a leak in the nearby firehouse. It was still manned, but there were threats of disbanding the companies until further notice. The guys in the house were up in arms, and rightly so.

One of the regular firefighters was stationed outside the front door. He wasn't letting just anybody in, and you had to show him your ID. Stories of guys losing their turnout gear or helmet to a scavenging souvenir hunter were enough to make anybody sick.

Out of the bathroom, I peeked my head into the kitchen. Nobody around. The place didn't seem like a firehouse any more. I'd worked there as a firefighter over ten years ago. We'd had several runs into Tower Two: same office, same faulty alarm, way up on the 40th floor. The officer had got a little stern with whoever was in charge, and I'd heard that the firms were charged a $250 fine by the city every time the Fire Department had to respond to a bogus alarm.

But now there was no fire engine there. No fire truck either.

I met a guy who escaped the falling towers and said that, afterwards, they'd brought some of the injured into the back of the firehouse. He hadn't known it was a firehouse, due to the dust everywhere. He thought it was a restaurant when he saw all the pots and pans hanging up on the overhead rack. This place wasn't going to be the same for a long while, perhaps a year or more.

Out front, I met a guy with a few spiral-bound manual books in his hands.

'Hey Lou, get a load of this!'

It was an anti-terrorism manual, and right smack in the middle of the front page was a drawing of the twin towers with a target site in red, like a sniper's rifle sight. It was unnerving to see that book again. I remembered when it was first printed, shortly after the first bombing back in '93.

One of the visiting 'Americans' from another state nosed in on what we were looking at. He took one of the manuals, handed it to me and said: 'Hey, y'all mind me takin' a picture, with you holdin' this?'

I said, very politely, 'Yes, I do mind,' handing the book back to him.

Man, I thought to myself, nothing is sacred around here. That kind of shit really bothered me.

My guys were looking pretty bored, so I told them some dirty jokes. 'They should call this "The Sit-Around Command Post",' one of them complained, but they were all still in good spirits.

By now two full companies had arrived. I knew one of the officers and tried to convince him to take over from us. He saw what we'd been doing all day and politely refused, which was kind of shitty, but I understood his viewpoint. Another team of firefighters made its way to the front of the trailer. The chief said that it looked as though he had three companies, so all of the daytime guys could go.

'You better hurry up too, or else you'll miss your bus.' We started out for Broadway. It was about five blocks, and there wasn't a bus in sight. We walked to the entrance of the Brooklyn Bridge, and stood about two blocks from the entrance ramp. Me and another guy took a walk up to a store to buy some beer. The day was over, I was thirsty and so were my men. They deserved a reward for all that hard work that they hadn't done.

After a few beers, I wasn't thinking so much about what had gone on in the last few days. It was getting to be a habit, and I knew it didn't really help – but for this last time, I told myself, it was the best I could do.

7

Day Two with Engine 37

I wasn't sleeping at all lately. My wife wasn't sleeping well either, as I was so restless, getting up several times during the night to cough my lungs up or get a drink. Sometimes I'd go out on the couch and read.

The book I was reading was *Bury My Heart at Wounded Knee* by Dee Brown, an American Indian. It was the true story of what happened in the American Midwest as early settlers came in and drove the Indians on to reservations. It was an atrocity, and it can never be denied that this country's native people were slaughtered in the name of a new and expanding America.

The story was so tragic that it took my mind off what was going on in New York. It made my problems look like a broken fingernail. I'm not trying to downplay what occurred, or revise it. But man has been demonstrating his inhumanity to man for thousands of years. It isn't until it happens in your own backyard that you gain some appreciation of its horror. Like my Israeli neighbour, Adam, said on the morning of the 11th: 'This is the way it is back in Israel, every day, it's crazy! People all over the world are suffering things like this every day. The perpetrators must be insane. Who would ever do such a thing?'

The word 'assassin' comes to mind. The word comes from the Arabic '*hashashin*', the plural form of '*hashash*', which means 'one who eats hashish'. In days gone by, nearly a thousand years ago, men who were all tanked up on this drug were told by the terrorist leader Hasan Bin Sabah that if they committed heinous crimes in the name of Allah, they would spend eternity in a place where rivers flowed with milk and honey and young virgins were at their beck and call. With this, the cult of the assassins was created. Sounds pretty sick, right? It's a story from the journals of Marco Polo, but it still rings true today.

The veneer of civilisation was eroded on September 11. It's time for the entire world to wake up, and consider that the human race, as a species, is bordering on the edge of extinction. Imagine how things might be if the same terrorists who committed those acts had nuclear weapons at their disposal.

The world is getting so small that wherever something happens, it impacts on everyone in the long run.

The Fire Department is a perfect example of how small the world really is. The last time I looked at the list of missing and fallen, I recognised a bunch of the guys I had taught at the Fire Academy back in 1998. They only had three-plus years in the Department. Now they were gone for ever, like so many other young guys. Men like them were the heart and soul of the Department, who learned on their very first day at the Academy what it really meant to be a New York City firefighter.

After I left the Academy, I'd run into these guys every now and then. I'd always keep a special eye out for them as, for the most part, they didn't have too much experience on the job, and I felt I owed it to them. I'm considering going back to the Fire Academy to train new recruits now. If I can relay to them what it's taken me my whole career to learn, I'll have really achieved something.

I was considering all this stuff as I was preparing myself to go to the World's Fair Arena, where we had to meet to go down to the site. The traffic was next to nothing, so I arrived at the parking lot well ahead of the other guys. I hoped we'd do some good work today. The other day had been pure bullshit.

I nodded off in the car for a short time, and then awoke feeling really tired. I'd got in the habit of wanting to sleep in all the wrong places. I forced myself to get up and stand outside the car, getting some fresh air.

Quite a few guys had arrived by this time. I must have slept for longer than I'd thought. I found my company, and we boarded a bus full of guys from Queens and the Bronx. The sun was beginning to come up, with various shades of orange mixed with the last vestiges of the night sky.

As we approached the drop-off point, in front of the Trinity Church, a lieutenant told us to wait for our assignments when we left the bus. Well, that put a damper on all my plans. I was told to take my men and go to the Vesey Street command station. Their spirits weren't at their best at that time in the morning, and I wasn't expecting them to go too much higher. These guys wanted to do something productive.

The day went by like this: hour by hour, the FEMA rescue teams scurried all over the Pile, while we just sat around and waited . . . It was a very foreign feeling to all of us, having to sit around and have some other agency deal with what we felt we could do ourselves. Some companies were employed down in the Pile, loading debris onto a metal scoop. The scoop would be lifted up by a crane and brought over to a cleared area where it would be dumped and sifted. The work these guys were doing was very limited, and it didn't look like they were going to need relief.

The three most used words in the Department are surely, 'We got it,' or, alternatively, 'I got it.' I was taught this positive attitude very early on, by the senior men in my company on the Lower East Side. But every time I went to the big tent to see what work we might be able to do, I was told the same thing: 'Just hang in there.'

Looking back, it's easier to understand that with this scale of tragedy, there was no battle plan and no one who really knew what the hell was going on. One thing was clear in my mind: we couldn't stand to lose any more guys. I'm sure this was what the brass were thinking, when they restricted the amount of men working in and on the Pile. It was a very dangerous site, and needed to be controlled to avoid more casualties.

At about 4.30 in the afternoon, I called my mother on a cell phone one of the guys let me use.

'Payroll,' she answered at the other end.

'Hey, Ma!' I greeted her.

'John?'

'Yeah, Ma, it's me.'

'How are you doing?'

I could feel the apprehension in her voice. We hadn't seen or spoken to each other for about a week, since the day of September 11.

'Mom, I'm down on Church and Vesey, come down and meet me at the corner of Liberty and Broadway.'

My mom was in charge of the payroll at the New York Stock Exchange, and I felt that if she wanted to take a break to see her son, it shouldn't be a problem.

When I told the guys I was going to see my mom, they razzed me as much as anyone would expect. I arrived at the corner of Broadway and Liberty Street, where we were meeting. There were soldiers there, giving the grim impression that New York City had been placed under martial law.

About ten minutes went by, before I saw her coming up the street. As I watched her, I couldn't help thinking of how small and frail she looked. This whole thing had taken a heavy toll on her. My mom had been working at the Exchange for the last thirty years and had never been through anything like this.

I could see the hurt and the concern in her eyes as she approached. There was a police barricade between us and I had to lean over it to embrace her.

'Oh John, I'm so glad to see you!' she said as I held her. There were small tears in the corners of her eyes.

She asked me what I was doing down there today, and I told her. She took a good look around and said, 'Things haven't changed much since that morning, it seems.'

'What time did you arrive here in the city that day, Ma?'

This was her opportunity to unload on me what she'd seen that morning.

Mom's Story

Approximately 20 million people travel on the Staten Island ferry every year. On September 11, 2001, I was one of those people.

I travel to Wall Street every working day, Monday to Friday. On that day, I was running a little late. There are many stories like mine.

Some of those who ran late are luckier than those who reached their desks early.

For those unfamiliar with New York, the ferry is the greatest way to commute to Manhattan. You go get your coffee, juice, doughnut, whatever. You read your paper, or your book, pay your bills, chat with friends. For some people it's a social gathering, sharing weekend adventures, talking about movies you saw, catching up on gossip. It's a relaxing way to get to work.

That morning I was reading my book, until I heard a man exclaim, 'Oh my God!' All of us passengers nearby looked up. We saw a skyscraper with flames shooting out of the upper floors. From where I was sitting, I didn't realise it was the World Trade Center – when you're in the harbour, approaching the tip of Manhattan, all the buildings blend into each other from a distance.

No one was overly concerned, it seemed to be just another fire in the city. The ferry docked, and we all left to go to our respective offices. But as I walked up Whitehall Street, I heard a plane. It was flying so low that when I looked up I thought, 'Is it going to land *here*?'

I didn't have time for another thought before it hit the World Trade Center and exploded.

Everyone around me was running and crying. It was sheer panic. Some returned to the ferry to go back home to Staten Island. I know it sounds strange, but I didn't feel too frazzled. I've lived in New York City all my life, seen a lot of crazy things, and just thought it was a freak accident. I carried on walking through the streets of lower Manhattan, as I've been doing for 31 years. I figured that when I got to my office I'd find out what was going on.

As I approached Broad Street, which is right in the middle of the hubbub of the financial centre, I saw people streaming back to where I'd just left. I didn't know what the heck was going on, but I noticed the street was full of debris. How could that plane have caused such a mess three or four long blocks away?

Stock Exchange workers wearing coloured jackets, with their firms' corporate insignia, were running down Broad Street. When I reached my building, my co-workers were standing on the street and informed me that the plane I'd seen had hit the World Trade Center.

All of the buildings that make up the concrete canyon of Wall Street had periodic fire drills. Representatives of FDNY explained what to do if there was a fire in your building: how to exit, how to notify the Department. There had never been a demonstration to explain what to do in the event of a terrorist attack. The employees who were in the building when the first plane hit said it felt like an explosion right next door, and we were located a full four blocks away from the WTC.

The debris from the impact of the plane was still falling all around. All the paper on the street looked like the aftermath of a happier time, a ticker-tape parade after the New York Yankees won the World Series.

As we were waiting to decide whether to go home, we were instructed that we could re-enter the building. Mind you, we still didn't know exactly what had happened, as we didn't have access to any communication from the media.

Inside, we tuned into the radio news and heard that another plane had hit the Pentagon. To say the least, we were all very concerned. *What on earth could happen next?*

We were told that it was all right for us to go back to work and that the matter would be handled by the emergency services of the city. Myself and my staff went up to our offices.

I tried to concentrate on my work, but I couldn't stop wondering what had happened at the WTC. Our firm occupied a couple of floors there. Had everyone managed to get out? Were they OK?

I shared my office with four co-workers, our work involving constant interaction. The office had six large windows that faced Broad Street.

We were trying to recover our composure when the building shook with a loud explosion. I looked out and saw a cloud of smoke covering all six windows. Thinking that our building was hit, I told everyone to get out of the office. The elevators were working, but, remembering the instructions for the fire drills, we all took the exit stairs to the lobby.

As we went down the stairs, dust was seeping in from the collapse of the first building. The lobby was no better. We all were trying to cover our mouths and faces with our clothing when we were told to go back to the stairways. It was a little better there, but not for long, and we were led to an area where the ventilation system was good.

Once we were there, we were able to see and hear on the TV what was going on outside. It was the most shocking event in the world. As I watched the TV, all I could think of was that my sons, who worked as a fireman and a policeman, my sons-in-law, my daughter-in-law, could be there, under the collapsed buildings. They were all 'on the job'. I started to cry, and my friend put her arm around me and tried to comfort me.

Eventually, I was able to contact my daughter on Staten Island and she told me everyone was OK. We had a medical office nearby to administer attention if needed, and there were a few minor situations – but nothing compared to what was happening outside.

We all just waited and waited. Hundreds of people not knowing what would happen next.

After about four hours of waiting, it was announced that we could leave the premises if we wished. The firm expressed their concerns for our safety, and co-workers pleaded with my friend and me to stay, but I just had to get home. We were handed wet cloths to help us breathe when we got outside the building.

When we opened the door, we couldn't believe what we saw.

It was like a science fiction movie.

The streets were littered with debris about a foot high. People were walking with masks on, trudging down the street like alien invaders. We made our way to the ferry, along with thousands of other people trying to get back to Staten Island. I'll remember that day for the rest of my life, and I'm sure everyone else there will too.

Months later, I still work on Wall Street. Every day, people still talk about what happened on September 11, 2001, and wonder how something like this could ever have occurred.

It's a changed world now – the other world, where we felt so safe and secure, is gone.

No one feels safe any more.

After she finished, we just stood there in silence. Many people walked by with cameras at their sides, stopping to take some shots when they hit the corner. I told her I had to get back before I was missed, though there were at least a hundred ready, willing and able firefighters down at the Vesey Street command.

I leaned over the blue police barricade and hugged and kissed my mom goodbye. I watched her as she faded into the river of people heading down Broadway.

As I made my way across Broadway, the soldiers didn't even look at me. The street was all torn up on either side, due to repairs in the electric lines and other utilities that serviced the WTC and surrounding buildings. The chain link fence went as far as I could see up Broadway, delineating the zone that was affected by the disaster. As I walked down the street I could see names scrawled out in the dust on the storefronts. People from all over the United States had something to say on each and every pane of glass along the way.

I hit Church Street and found my crew at the Sit-Around Command Post. They were looking more bored than ever. I went back to the tent and asked the chief if he had anything for my guys to do.

'Well, we're going to be moving this whole operation across the street in about fifteen minutes, we'll need all hands at that point, get 'em ready.'

'You're shittin' us, right?' came their response when I told them.

'I shit you not,' I said. They perked up a bit, and we all headed over to where things were starting to be taken apart. The tent was a big one, and had sixteen poles or more that held it up. There were at least two guys on each pole and we walked the whole thing across the street and put it down intact, just like it was set up when we started. It was a well coordinated effort, if I say so myself. Then the chief told me to take my men and go to the bus, we were done for the day.

Soon there were a hundred other firefighters waiting as well. We were all from the same area and everyone knew one another, like one big family. It was a crowded ride to the World's Fair Arena, and I couldn't wait to get off the bus.

We arrived at the parking lot about a half hour later. We all undressed and stowed our gear in the trunks of our cars. A few of the guys put their gear into plastic garbage bags, to prevent it from contaminating their cars or bringing whatever was down at the site home to their families.

We all said goodbye in the belief we'd see one another in three days' time, as we now had 48 hours off.

We didn't know it, but the World Trade Center task force would be restructured after our tour and none of us would go back down there again – unless it was as a volunteer.

I sat down in my car after saying my goodbyes and had a quiet moment to myself. Memories of my old captain, and spending a day with him in the Catskill Mountains at an Irish music festival, came back to me.

It was in September 1997 that he'd told me about the fair and I'd taken a ride up there. I'd returned from a trip to Ireland about three weeks previously and was still feeling very Irish, having traced my roots. I'd brought back a piece of 'peat' or 'turf' (soil), as they call it across the pond. I'd given it to him, not knowing the significance of it. He was very thankful for it, so much that I wondered what the big deal was. When I went to the Irish festival I met with his wife, who I hadn't seen in a few years. Then I found out the significance of the peat.

It turned out that the captain's mother-in-law had passed away not too long before, and, as she originated from Ireland, they placed a piece of peat in the coffin with her. Now another piece of native soil was coming back from Ireland to them.

I dozed off for about a half hour, and was woken by the sound of an airplane flying just a bit too low for comfort. I started the car and headed home to where I hoped I'd be able to get some sleep.

8

Day Tour in Midtown

After my second tour on the WTC task force, other men were assigned to Ground Zero and I was back in the field. One of my first assignments was with Engine 54, in the heart of midtown Manhattan, who share their headquarters with Ladder 4 and Battalion 9 as well. These companies are among the busiest on the job.

On the apron of Engine 54's front door it was like a funeral home, with at least a hundred people paying their respects to the fifteen firefighters they had lost – one third of the firehouse. Being located in the middle of the theatre district, the firehouse is visited by many of the tourists who come to NYC. Every time the rigs pull out the front door, cameras snap off shots of New York's bravest in action.

After the 11th, the amount of visitors had grown astronomically. It was only 8.30 and the crowd was already beginning to swell. There wasn't any way we could shut the door and pretend to be closed, after all. Instead, the men met the public out on the apparatus floor, grateful for whatever gifts were thrust in our faces. It was mirrored at every firehouse in the city, only here it seemed more pronounced. Bouquets of flowers came in by the hour, so many that a local lady volunteered her time for the job of handling them all. The front of the firehouse was covered with flowers, and more than two hundred candles. Above them was a photo of all the guys who perished on the 11th; below them a seven-foot replica of the Statue of Liberty. People from all over the world stopped in to sign a book of condolence, in which they could leave their own personal messages.

From out of the crowd, a woman approached me with a bag of buttons. On one side of the buttons was screenprinted the image of a red, white and blue ribbon, twisted into a figure eight lying on its side. Underneath it was the legend, 'Unbroken'. 'This is the new symbol for the New York City tourist board,' she said. 'See this symbol?' She showed me the ribbon design. 'This means infinity.'

I took the bag of buttons and thanked her. At roll call, I handed them out to each man, and some of the guys put them on their helmets. It was just another day at the firehouse for all of us, but for the public it had some more symbolic significance.

Everything you can imagine came in through the front door in the way of gifts, to all the firehouses. All sorts of teddy bears, for example – I'd never heard of 'bear therapy' before, but there were more than enough bears for every firefighter. Usually, visitors would buy T-shirts with the firehouse logo on them. However, there weren't any more left now that the firehouse had become a tourist attraction. The guys would sometimes get tired of this, and occasionally shut the front door to get a break from the endless stream of visitors.

In the front of the firehouse, on the ground floor, right off the side of the apparatus floor, there was this little room where the guys could watch TV or do whatever they wanted. They had a video game set up. It was a Second World War scenario where the player had to make his way through German-occupied territory to accomplish some task or other. One firefighter, Mike Haub, had been able to speak German, and they would turn up the sound so he could interpret what the soldiers were saying and tell everyone what was going on. I'd taught Haub at the Fire Academy back in 1998 – but now, he was one of the missing guys whose photos were out in front of headquarters. The little room was rapidly filling up with donated gifts, and no one played the video game any more.

The other regular officer was busy all day visiting the widows and families, doing whatever he could to assuage their grief and handle some of the affairs that sprang up in the wake of a major tragedy. It was like this in every firehouse. One or two other guys were also assigned to the task of helping out the families. It was a very burdensome job, but no one was heard to complain.

Every time I went into the office, I'd see the stack of photos of guys who had worked here. Their pictures had previously been neatly framed and affixed to the board, but as is customary when someone dies or transfers, their pictures were taken down. Everything was happening too fast. It was bad enough when one guy died, now we were dealing with three hundred-plus who were no longer with us. It was staggering just to think about it.

There was so much going on that day, and the phone rang non-stop. But it was mostly enquiries from the families and other firehouses, and although we had about eight runs, none of them amounted to anything. Later on, Lieutenant Bob Jackson came back from all of the visits he'd had to make, and told me he wanted to take over as officer and ride on the fire engine for the rest of the night. I didn't have any qualms about it, knowing how much pride he placed in his company. So I hit the sack and managed to get four or five hours' sleep.

When I awoke the next morning, the day seemed just like a carbon copy of the day one. Out front, the crowds still thronged around. As I pushed through, making the way across the street to my car, as a firefighter I attracted stares of both curiosity and concern.

First Day at Pier 94

In early October, about three weeks after September 11, I was assigned to the Family Assistance Center located on Pier 94. I was told to report to the pier early in the morning in my Class A uniform. The place was at least 2,000 feet long and another 1,000 feet across, perhaps bigger. It was the size of several football fields, whichever way you looked at it. There was a seemingly endless amount of booths set up to advise the anticipated crowd of bereaved relatives on what financial support they were entitled to.

It was the first day that it was possible to obtain a death certificate for a missing loved one, even if no remains had been found yet. A lot of people were expected to arrive, due to the fact that nothing could be done for anyone until they held the death certificate in their hand.

I found the desk with the Fire Department representatives. There were two computer monitors set up at our table, one showing the site that had all the data on every firefighter who had died. There was a photo of each guy, the date when he came on the job, and some personal data. The screen saver on the computer was a photo of people trapped above the burning floors high up in the twin towers. From the expressions on their faces, it seemed they were bracing themselves to jump. It was a pretty damn morbid thing to have as a screen saver. I took it all in one more time, before vowing to myself that I wouldn't look at it any more that day.

There was something very cold and distant about the whole place, and I didn't feel comfortable there. Everything had to do with bottom-line material benefits. People who came there would walk away with specified amounts of money, depending on the nature of their relationship with a person who had died at the WTC. All the big-gun charity organisations were there in force: the Red Cross, the Salvation Army, Victims of Crime. They had numerous booths set up, and plenty of staff to interview people who came in seeking assistance.

No one was dealing with the more meaningful or spiritual aspects of bereavement at all. All the same, while money is not the main thing in life (it's not even close), the material aspects surely had to be dealt with. I knew a lot of the guys who had died worked additional jobs just to make ends meet. I still needed to moonlight once in a while, and, at one point, had depended on a moonlight job to pay many of the bills that came into my household.

There were about ten agencies offering assistance altogether. One of them was an Oriental philosophical organisation giving out checks for $1,000 to anyone who could prove they were directly related to the deceased. In addition to all the financial support offered, the FBI were handling any travel costs involved in bringing relatives to New York to attend the funeral of a loved one. They picked up the hotel bills as well – for an impersonal government bureaucracy, it was pretty impressive.

The first widow came in, and was introduced to us. I told the others that I'd take care of her, as I'd worked with her husband. I took her around to all of the agencies, waiting for her to get through the endless paperwork. She kept it together throughout the whole time as we went around all the different booths. As the day wore on, however, it became apparent that some of the agencies were just dead ends.

After it was all done, I told her I'd known her husband, and related a story about him. He'd mistakenly left a tool at a location where we'd just responded to an emergency. All the guys were razzing him about it and he felt really bad. Then the phone rang and he answered it. Someone on the other end said they'd found a tool in the basement and were going to bring it to the firehouse. We were standing out front when he told me and another guy about the call. The other firefighter said, 'Oh, you've at least got to buy the guy a shirt.' He looked kind of embarrassed, and agreed, 'Yeah, that makes sense.' So he went to the back locker and bought one of the company T-shirts that people came in off the street to buy. He was standing there waiting for the guy to bring the tool back when someone asked who it was for. He told the story to a crowd of guys, and got a resounding, 'Are you shittin' me?'

'You mean to say somebody called you and told you that they were going to drive all the way over here to bring the tool back, and you believed them?' someone asked, in a very sarcastic tone of voice. All he could do was to say yes. One of the 'wise men' (every firehouse has its wise men, and its 'professors' – they'll offer you their professional opinion on anything and everything) asked if it occurred to him that maybe someone had used the payphone on the second floor to call up the departmental phone.

I'd started to feel sorry for the poor guy. He was standing there holding the T-shirt he'd just paid for, waiting for someone who might never show up, and the other guys were razzing him no end.

I waited with him for about a half hour. I was about to give up, and go start the paperwork entailed in losing Fire Department property, when a car pulled up on the apron out front. The driver didn't have anything in his hands, so it looked like he was just going to ask for directions. Then he stopped at the trunk and pulled out the tool. The look of relief and gratitude on the face of the firefighter was something to behold, and I was glad for him. When I finished telling his widow this story, she smiled gently and thanked me.

The captain told two of us to take a break as it was coming up to lunchtime. As we walked over to the food hall we talked about what we'd experienced emotionally over the past two weeks. It was kind of weird to have this conversation with another firefighter, but welcome all the same. I told him about the first time I'd cried after the 11th. He told me, 'Wow, it took me almost a week.' We were all so stoical, I thought. It took such a lot for us to even admit we were upset, on account of our conditioning. One thing was for sure – all the razzing in the kitchen hadn't done anything to enhance anyone's sensitivity.

But it was uncomfortable for me to be with these women when I'd known or worked with their spouses. They looked so helpless as they approached the desk. Everything they'd once known was gone; all the dreams of their future had been wiped out for ever one morning in September.

The venue was just one giant financial flea market. To call it anything else is an insult to the human spirit. The only real solace offered came in the form of a cheque. We all felt the same way about that cold, impersonal place, and that there should be more information available for our people before they arrived, to make it easier on them. It was decided that we should split up and go around to every appropriate booth. With a newfound determination, I made my way around to the four booths on my list and found out what was required as far as ID and marriage certificates were concerned.

I got all the help possible, and everyone was incredibly cooperative. Usually, with city agencies, there was so much red tape it was a wonder anything got done at all. Mayor Giuliani's office had thrown all this together; they were doing a tremendous job in the light of all that had occurred. Some people found it easy to criticise, and talked as if they could do a better job, but I didn't see them running for office.

In fact, the guys who were missing were still getting a paycheque every two weeks, plus overtime. It was only money, I know, but it could so easily have gone the other way.

I was taking down the information from each booth to make out a sheet with all the pertinent details. This sheet would be faxed to all the divisions, who would fax it to all the battalions in turn, who would then fax it to every firehouse in the city. This would ensure that it got to any widows or families who needed the information. It was a relatively small job, but it was crucial when it came to taking care of one another.

Another widow came in, with her father. She'd given birth around a week ago and had made it all go right out of sheer force of will. She knew she'd still have to come in and try to sort this whole mess out, and now she was getting teary-eyed when certain questions were asked. All I could think of was my wife at home, and how she'd have had to deal with this had I arrived down at Ground Zero ten minutes earlier. If I'd made it down there in time, I'd probably have been close enough to get caught in the collapse. When they're young, most people have a feeling that they're invincible or immortal. But even for anyone still young enough to labour under this illusion, September 11 was going to be a permanent wake-up call from now on.

Around 10.30, the last caller, a young woman, walked up to the table. 'My boyfriend was a firefighter and we were living together. Where do I have to go?' Thankfully, all she had to do was show some evidence that they shared the same living space, or had mutual bank accounts, and there wouldn't be any problems for her.

The captain was almost done putting the divisional fax together. Now the fun began. We had to fax all this stuff through. Most, maybe all, of us would have much rather been running into a burning tenement than doing this. I sent out the faxes to all of the divisions and waited about fifteen minutes, then called them all to ensure they had received it. This took another hour or so. I told some of the other guys to go as it was after midnight, and it didn't look like anyone was coming in that late. I was planning to stay till about 2 a.m., and then I was cutting out. In about an hour, every firehouse had received the fax.

I felt like I'd really accomplished something that day – and maybe I had.

Smoke from WTC 1 drifts over the steel I-beams littering the whole of West Street, moments after the collapse of WTC 7.

The remains of WTC 1, with the ladders that were used to gain access. This is where many of the fallen firefighters were carried down in body bags, which were laid in baskets and guided down the ladders.

A piece of WTC 1, embedded in the building across the street.

The collapsed Vesey Street walkway is visible in the top right corner. The front of Ladder 5 can be seen on the left.

Standing on top of what is referred to as the 'cantilever' at the edge of the crater. The crushed atrium between the two World Financial Centers can be seen in the distance, having been hit by the falling WTC 1.

The north face of WTC 7. At this time on September 11, the south side was fully engulfed in flames.

The burned, crushed remains of WTC 5.

Looking out over the ruins from the Church Street side (note the World Financial Center in the background).

9

Eddy Day's Memorial

It was 2 p.m., October 6. I reached Sailor Snug Harbor in Staten Island, where Eddy Day's funeral was being held. I'd worked with Ed back when I was in Engine 28 on Manhattan's Lower East Side.

I'd been here just four months ago, to attend my brother's wedding – in an old clump of buildings on a huge piece of land at the edge of Staten Island, straight across from New Jersey. It was a home for retired sailors, harking back to the days when the high seas were the only gateway to the world abroad. All the little houses where they used to live were preserved landmarks, and there were several other larger buildings where I imagined they held dances, meetings and other social events. Then there was the chapel, where my brother got married.

The service for Eddy was being held in the Great Hall, a larger assembly place. I was dressed in my best gear, as was everyone else. Heading off to where they were all assembled, I passed a children's museum where I remembered taking my kids when they were small. As I got closer, I saw all the familiar faces.

They all seemed a little older, perhaps a little greyer. There were a lot of hands to shake, and everyone wanted to catch up on all the years since we'd last seen each other. Most of these guys were from the surrounding companies that worked close to Engine 28 and Ladder 11 – like Tom Sullivan, who gave me a big smile and shook my hand. I remembered when Tom first came to Engine 28, when I'd had about three years on the job and thought I was hot stuff. I'd shown him around on the first day he arrived, and took great pride in doing so. It was the first time I'd been allowed to tell a new

119

firefighter what was expected of him in the Department, and it made me feel a real sense of purpose and belonging. But now Tom and I were pretty much lost for words.

The order came to fall into line. We were getting used to doing this at memorial and funeral services, what with all the practice we'd been having. We made a short order of it and were all looking pretty sharp. Civilian mourners were milling around the entrance to the Great Hall, starting to spill out of the doorway. Music started to play from hidden speakers – the rock and roll group REM, with their saddest song, 'Everybody Hurts'. I couldn't believe they were playing this song. I recalled hearing it back in the early nineties, when I was going through my divorce, and how it had torn me up. Now I was feeling pain all over again – and so was everyone else.

Eddy's widow came out first, escorted by Bobby Alverson. Bobby had been helping to take care of the families of all the guys who died in Ladder 11 and Engine 28, like John Heffernan.

We all stood rigidly to attention as the music played softly. It was like something from a movie, unfolding in slow motion. Tears welled up at the corner of my eyes and the emotion mounted up inside me. I wasn't the only one – in my field of vision, I could see a few guys getting teary-eyed.

How much more of this could we take? This was what it must have been like to go to war and lose some of your good buddies. As if to emphasise it, as the music faded away there was a trumpet player starting to play 'Taps' the stark and moving military tune traditionally played at funerals.

The family walked on up past the formation of men to the waiting cars. In between the trumpet notes all we heard were their footsteps, and the fallen leaves as they blew across the pavement, signifying a full stop in the cycle of life.

The last note faded into the autumnal atmosphere that arrived with the setting of the sun. I watched people's eyes as they drifted by in their cars, all affected so deeply in their own way by what had happened. I thought of Eddy, whose wife was German and who used to teach me some of the German language I'd long since forgotten from high school, and of all the little memories of friendship that everyone was carrying around of people that we'd lost.

A crowd of relatives and friends were gathering at a local social hall called the Pavilion. It had been around since the 1800s, and I'd been to half a dozen weddings there over the years. In fact, it was the place where I'd attended my first prom.

The order 'Company dismissed' was given, and we were free to do as we pleased. One of the guys from Engine 28 whom I hadn't seen in years gave me a big hug. It was like coming home. I'd spent some of the best years of my life with these guys.

'Hey McCole! Are you coming over to the gathering?'

'Yeah!' I hollered across. We all took off to our cars. I was a little overwhelmed after seeing all these old faces. It was like I'd stepped back in time ten years. Nothing had changed, it was like I'd never left. It felt great to be welcomed back.

My elation didn't last. In my car, I started to think about the other funerals going on right then. Of all the widows who had to be consoled. I could hear the fatherless kids talking among themselves, trying to understand why Daddy wasn't coming home. My emotions were building up to some kind of peak, and it all came out of me.

I sat there and wept. It felt good. I knew I needed to get it out. I get a funny kind of pain in my chest when I've been exposed to a lot of grief. One time, I thought it was because I had a heart condition. Then I would have a good cry and it'd go away, like magic. I guess that was where the term 'broken heart' came from, an actual physical manifestation in the chest. Nowadays, I accepted the need to cry as long as I was in a situation where I felt safe and secure.

I looked at my eyes to check they weren't too red. 'Oh, who gives a shit anyway? We've *all* been crying!' I found a spot to put my car outside the parking lot, which was a sea of confusion. It was just like the parking areas at most firehouses I'd worked in – they jammed eleven cars into a space only designed for eight. It was quite an art, but it meant the guys could always get a job parking cars when they retired.

At the Pavilion, I wanted a drink to help me relax a little. The bar was packed with guys from 28 and 11, and it was just like old times. Someone put a Budweiser down in front of me and the night began. We were all drinking, laughing it up, trying to have a good time. But there was an obvious dark cloud over us. For my part, I didn't think we'd seen even half of the misery that resulted from what occurred on the 11th.

Somebody was going around collecting medals, insignia, collar pins and bars to give to one of the widows as tokens of affection and remembrance. I gave up one of my lieutenant's bars – what the hell, I'd have to find a new one somewhere.

I had had a couple of drinks and decided it was a good idea to get some food inside me. Some ham, a few pieces of chicken Marsala, a roll, and a few stuffed mushrooms were good for now. I took my food back to the bar, where I received another old blast from the past. It was Joey Brennan, who was all smiles and as far gone as me with regard to alcohol content.

'How's it goin', John? Hey man, long time no see! Shit, you're lookin' good!'

I said likewise, but then Joe lowered his voice and spoke without moving his mouth very much. You could always tell he was getting serious when he spoke like that. 'Man, this is fucked up. It's two months, right, and I still can't believe it. So many guys, gone.' His voice trailed away.

'Yeah, Joe,' I said, 'we haven't seen the beginning of it yet. Imagine what everybody's going to feel like after all the funerals are over. After all the candles and flowers are gone. Then we're gonna see some upset people. Everyone's busy now, burying the dead. It's when we're alone with our own thoughts that the troubles begin.

'After the Oklahoma City bombing, where not one rescue worker was killed or seriously injured, the divorce rate among the cops and firefighters tripled. Drug and alcohol use went up, and the suicide rate increased as well. What do you think will happen here?'

I didn't let him answer. I was on a roll. 'People say, "Oh well, there's counselling for this type of thing." But they had counselling down in Oklahoma, right? It didn't help much down there. There needs to be a new approach to the human mind. The mental health field is too hand in glove with the pharmaceutical industry. If you go to the shrink and tell him you're feeling depressed, he gives you a prescription; if you tell him you're anxious, he gives you a prescription. How about seeing what the guy is eating, who he's hanging around with? Get to know the guy first. There's a whole range of alternatives to just treating the symptoms with drugs. But there's a vested interest in keeping things the way they are. If anything is gonna change, the change has to come from us.'

I don't know if he heard anything I said. So maybe I was talking too much. Going into too much depth can make some people uncomfortable. But everything starts with a thought. Take a good look around you. Most of what you see had to be created in somebody's mind before it was realised in the material world.

People were starting to leave, and it was getting late. I used to be one of those guys who had to be chased out after the last round. At three or four o'clock in the morning, when all the ugly girls had been scooped up and the bartender was putting chairs up on the bar, it used to be time for me to leave.

Things were different now, and I was usually home before midnight. I guess I was getting older – maybe even wiser.

I said my goodbyes and somehow managed to get home – to my mom's, that is. I'd already called my wife, and she'd given me a piece of her mind about my being drunk and how I shouldn't be driving so I thought it best I stayed at mom's. Truth be told, I was feeling just a little bit out of it. These funerals, combined with all the alcohol and meeting a load of my old friends, had done a real number on me.

Something had to change if I was going to get through this period of my life.

10

Night Tour on 29th Street

I had to work a night tour on 29th Street in Engine 16 and Ladder 7. It was mid-October. I'd worked there before, and was used to all the guys and the way the place ran. I'd last stopped off there a few days previously with my son, Bryce. He'd recently turned one year old, on September 3, and I was playing Mr Mom for the day.

When I walked into the firehouse that day, I was confronted by a firefighter who wanted to know who I was. He was pretty much in my face, and he was kind of scary.

When he'd confirmed my identity, he calmed down and became a little friendlier. He told me that he used to work there, but had retired from the Department less than a year ago. All the same, nine guys from that firehouse hadn't come home after the 11th, and he was pretty upset about it.

'I'm coming back,' he told me. 'Yeah, I called Personnel. It's no problem. So I've got to go for retraining. What's that?...a week? Man, I have to come back,' he underlined. 'Do you know how sick this makes me feel? I worked with all these guys – shit, I still can't believe it. You know what I mean?' I could tell he was off in his head somewhere, but I understood.

I'd brought both of my daughters to that same firehouse for a day tour during the summer before the 11th. Laura and Susie were aged thirteen and eleven respectively. They'd spent the day being entertained by a firefighter named George Cain, even while I took a nap (I'd had a bad night with the baby). The girls had taken turns riding on the trucks when we had to go out on a run, and had really loved it. George had since perished.

124

When I returned to the firehouse in late September, there were numerous poster boards featuring photos of the guys who had died, captured at functions and parties over the years. Written tributes had also been left by their fellow firefighters, and visitors who'd come to pay their respects.

The picture of Lieutenant Vernon Richards brought back to me his customary greeting of 'Hey, Big Guy,' when I came in to relieve him. Vern was a really warm human being, who always had an ear to listen if I was having any kind of difficulties I needed to talk through.

I'd tried to tell my girls what had happened to George Cain, and a few of the other guys they'd met on the day they visited. I'm not sure if they were able to take it all in – perhaps they needed to get a little older before they grasped the significance of how every one of us is mortal.

Back on night tour in Engine 16, the phone was ringing off the hook. The guys were all busy talking about arrangements for funerals and memorials, the whole nine yards.

'Hey Lou!' one of them called to me. 'We gotta go to an auction tonight.'

He only seemed half serious, so I dismissed what he was saying. I was in the office next to the house watch, trying to make sense of all the paperwork that was blowing in like a snowstorm, when some guy walked in and asked, 'Mickey here?' He was looking for Lieutenant Mickey Cross, a regularly assigned officer. I politely told him he was off that night.

'Oh, OK. Well, hey, my name is Ricky Byrd, and I live over across the street. I stop over here all the time.'

He told me he was on his way to one of the Yankee playoff games. I asked him where he was sitting. 'Oh, shit, I've got great seats! Yeah, I'm right on the rail. Third base, it's gonna be great!'

I was struck by an idea. 'Would you like a banner to hang out during the game that says, "Go Yanks", or something corny like that?'

When he answered, 'Yeah, that would be cool,' I said to the guys, 'Hey, let's whip up a banner for Ricky here, and maybe we'll see him on TV tonight. Be sure to put the company numbers on it.' They created a great banner out of some leftover WTC spray-paint and an old, faded, washed-out bedsheet.

The guys themselves had a lot of stuff lined up for that night. The first thing they had planned was to attend a memorial party fund-raiser for Tom McCann, who had been the battalion aide to the chief. It was being held at a bar not too far from headquarters, and we would be available via the departmental radio should we need to respond to a call. When we arrived at the bar on Second Avenue, there were Fire Department rigs all over the place. There was a twenty-dollar fee at the door, but when the bouncer saw who we were he just waved us in.

The place was packed with people: lots of civilians, firefighters both off duty and on duty. It was a sacred event – the first informal gathering this firehouse had had since the 11th. Behind the bar there were several big TV screens playing a video of Tom McCann.

As I walked down the length of the bar, I saw a deputy chief overcome with emotion and weeping openly. I felt I should do something, like pat him on the back or give him a hug – but it seemed too patronising, so I left him to his personal grief. He was fully dressed in ceremonial uniform, having just come back from a funeral for one of the local guys.

On the screen we viewed photos of Tom McCann throughout his life, and everyone went quiet. I ran into the 10th Battalion aide, whose name was John but we all called him Jocko. He was a very witty guy, and, unlike many of the others, seemed to be feeling no pain. 'You know, I love this fuckin' job,' he announced unasked. 'I really mean it. I've got 31 years on, and I'm not looking to quit anytime soon.'

He talked about all the guys who had perished in Ladder 13 and Engine 22. I appreciated his company, but the conversation was making me a little uncomfortable. I ran into the company I was working with, who had met up with off-duty guys from their firehouse and were talking about the events of the next day – a memorial mass was planned.

When we arrived back at the firehouse, the guys went into the kitchen to make dinner from some food donations. It was only a short while before they told me we had to go out and take care of something else. Once again, the dispatcher would send out any calls via our computer screen, positioned in the front of the rig where the officer and chauffeur sat.

I asked the driver where we were going, but he was just there for the night, like myself, and didn't have a clue. About three blocks from the firehouse we pulled over just ahead of where some very beautiful women happened to be standing. I was starting to think something fishy was going on. The guys were all out of the rig, and I was right on their tails.

One of them said, 'Didn't we tell you earlier? We're going to an auction, it's a fund-raiser. There's a bunch of broads inside and they're going to be auctioning off firemen. It's just a goof. The owner asked us if we'd come on over. She's a real nice lady.'

I was sold. It sounded like harmless fun. The junior man sat out in the rig, while we went to check out the evening's agenda. As we walked in, the patrons gave us a tremendous round of applause. At the rear of the bar there were a lot of off-duty firefighters hanging out, and women all over the place. *God almighty!* The bartender offered us some beers, but we all politely refused – we could only push it so far, after all. The bidding was to begin in a few minutes, but, beforehand, the owner was going to do a little number for us all.

She came out in a very slinky crimson dress that looked like it had been painted on. The music started to play, a classic striptease accompaniment but with a jazzier rhythm to it. She belted out the tune, and everyone was singing along with her. All of a sudden, three of my guys were right up there with her, screaming into the microphone. It was good to see them loosen up and have some fun, after all that had happened.

After the song was over, the owner shooed them back to the sidelines. She stood on a little stage area created for the occasion, and announced the first firefighter to come on up. The bidding had officially opened. A guy from the company came on wearing a muscle shirt, and the women went crazy! Some were screaming at the top of their lungs, and the owner quieted them all down with a steady 'Sshhh.'

'OK, ladies, let's put your mouths where – oops, oh I'm sorry! That must have been a little Freudian slip!'

There was a small chuckle from the crowd. 'Let me give you that again, girls: C'mon ladies, and put your money where your mouths are! There, I got it out right that time!'

'A hundred dollars!' screamed a woman at the back.

'One-fifty!' another cried out.

'Wow,' I thought to myself, 'this might actually add up to something.'

Four hundred and fifty dollars later, some older broad walked away with the young firefighter. It was all for fun, nothing serious, just a bunch of people having a few drinks and a good time.

They auctioned off eight more guys, raising about $3,000. Towards the end, the visiting chauffeur Billy Holland was dragged up on stage. The guys were breaking his balls because he was not one to smile very easily, and I didn't think he'd take it too well. But he surprised all of us, making a great job of entertaining the ladies with a few choice sarcastic remarks. After he was successfully auctioned off, he gave the obligatory hug and kisses to the old broad who bought him. Then we were out of there, the patrons cheering us again as we walked out.

Back at quarters, the phone was still going non-stop. There were numerous requests about the location and time of the next day's funeral, and the memorial service at the end of the week. Families needed to do something. Two months had gone by and most of their loved ones hadn't been found yet, so a memorial service was a way of seeking closure. The only drawback was that, if and when the remains were eventually found, the need for a proper burial would dredge up all the raw emotions again. It would all seem like it happened yesterday, and there would be little relief for those who were suffering.

After about ten minutes, the alarm bells told everybody to respond to a report of leaking gas. 'Everybody goes, turn out for an odour of ass,' announced the watch over the intercom system. It gave us all a chuckle – sometimes the oldest jokes are the best. We went roaring down the street, the wrong way against the traffic, with the siren and air horn blasting everything in sight. I liked to think of the air horn as being like the 'photon torpedoes' on *Star Trek* – when a car didn't get out of the way I just gave him a blast, and ninety-nine per cent of them would melt away.

The address we were responding to was only three blocks away and we were first on the scene. There was a building maintenance man waiting at the kerb. 'It was just a stove leaking gas out the back of the connection. I shut off the gas and disconnected the stove,' he reassured us. The ladder company still checked it out for themselves. After the 11th, nothing was ever taken for granted any more.

The rig bounced along the street, not taking the bumps too well. The usual fire engine was being decontaminated, due to all the dust it was exposed to down at Ground Zero. As we pulled up to the front of quarters, there was a huge bunch of people gathered. 'Hello sir, we're all visiting,' announced an Irish brogue, 'and we wanted to stop in and present your fire station with a donation from the people back home.'

They had come from Paddy Reilly's Pub, not more than fifty feet from the front door of the firehouse. It was as close to an Irish pub as could be found in New York, with emerald green furnishings and nothing but Guinness on tap. They all wandered into the firehouse with us, at least twenty of them. With a few kind words, their spokesman presented a cheque for $5000 to the senior man in the engine – the same firefighter who had recently been reinstated. He got a little emotional, then recomposed himself with a few strong, well-chosen words – giving voice to the gutsy tradition that New York City is built upon. I'm not ashamed to say it gave me goosebumps.

I managed to speak with a few folks from Donegal, who invited me to stay at their house should I ever visit Ireland again. After the crowd went back to the bar, I went upstairs to see if I could get some sleep. Sleep didn't come easy these days. If it wasn't the baby at home, then it was the running of the firehouse; if it was neither of those, then it was the voices in my head, all shouting for my attention – 'the committee', you might call them.

I still hadn't had a good night's sleep since the 11th. Just when things began to get quiet, it seemed like it was starting all over again. I hadn't even handled any of our financial bills in over a month. I had to change the way I was operating, or nothing in my life was going to get any better.

Luckily, it was a quiet night. Despite all the thoughts in my head, sleep eventually came like it always does – just as the sun began to rise. The relieving officer gently knocked on the door, but all I wanted to do was stay in bed. I'd briefly achieved a deep sleep, a good two, maybe even three hours.

As I drove home, I was suddenly overcome with emotion, thinking about one of the guys I used to work with.

It was difficult to push this stuff out of my mind, and it seemed the only thing that accomplished any relief was alcohol. I knew it was very far from a viable solution, so I was going to have to take steps towards helping myself.

When I got home, strangely enough, there was a message on the answer machine from a woman I'd known for some years. She was trained to deliver the techniques laid out in the book *Dianetics*, which was written back in the early fifties by L Ron Hubbard – a controversial figure who, nonetheless, had conducted a lot of research into what makes people tick. I'd made use of Dianetics before, and knew that it worked – although it required an individual to work very hard, and it could be very upsetting at times. But I'd had good results in the past, when I had to deal with my divorce, or with deaths in the family.

She'd left a number and I returned the call. I got her answer machine and left a very brief message. 'That's good enough,' I thought to myself, 'I really don't feel like addressing this today.'

Help is Possible...

Back when I was 21, I wasn't dealing with life very well. My mom and dad separated when I was just turning nineteen and it had a profound effect on me. I didn't want to accept the fact that this was way that my life was going to go. I became very depressed at times and turned to drugs and alcohol to change the way I felt. But things just got worse and when my father saw what was occurring, he told me to go and see a friend of his. According to my father, this guy was sort of a 'Wise Man' and could offer a different viewpoint on life in general.

I drove all the way out to the far end of Staten Island. Once I found the address I was looking for, I got out and rang the bell and waited for a response. A man came to the door and welcomed me into his house. His name was Chuck McSorley and he'd been a firefighter with my dad. He was in the later stages of leukaemia – though I didn't know this when I arrived, I just knew that he was sick and hadn't been feeling too well lately.

Chuck opened the door and invited me into the living room. 'Let's go down into the basement,' he said, 'do you want a beer?' I thought this strange, and I just said no. He took a beer from the fridge and we both went down below.

Now we were in his workshop – every good homeowner in Staten Island has a workshop. He asked me, 'So, what's up?'

I immediately looked for an excuse not to talk, coming to the conclusion that I didn't even know why I was there. He knew, however, and he wasn't going to let me off easy. Cutting right to the chase, he told me, 'You know, I'll tell you a story. About six years ago, the doctors gave me six months to live. They told me, "You better get your affairs in order, Mr McSorley, as you don't have much more time...perhaps six months at best." But ya know, here I am six years later, and I'm still around. Around 25 years ago I read this book. It changed the way I looked at things. You could say it changed my life. And that is the reason I'm still alive today. The name of the book was *Dianetics*.' That was all he said.

He died about eight months later. The cancer finally caught up with him. I didn't find out until after he died that he'd been in the Marines in the early fifties and participated as a volunteer in atomic weapons testing in the Yucca Flats. He was exposed to nuclear explosions approximately three miles from Ground Zero, standing in trenches over which the atomic wave would pass.

After he passed away, every time I saw the book *Dianetics*, I'd think of Chuck and what he had said about it. I picked it up a few times with the best intentions, but would put it down after reading the first twenty or thirty pages. It was hard, because it had a lot of words I didn't know the definitions of. Thinking I could figure out each word based on the context of how it was used, I ended up not knowing what the hell L. Ron Hubbard was trying to say. So I put it down, promising to read it with a dictionary one fine day.

Well, after about three unsuccessful tries, and eight years later, I sat down with a dictionary one day at the firehouse in 1990. It was the first of a number of sessions in which I'd sit reading it in the study room until I fell asleep, keeping a pillow nearby. I had to look up a lot of words, but at least I'd overcome my laziness. In fact, the very first page of the book tells the reader to make sure they don't go past any words they don't understand, and promises that only misunderstanding and incomprehension await those who do.

I read the book in between runs at the firehouse, and realised there was definitely something to it. I looked for an organisation in the city that might tell me more about the philosophy of Dianetics, found a branch of the Church of Scientology on the Upper East Side, and went in for an interview. It was decided that I would benefit from 'auditing' – the Scientologists' term for therapy, as the person who listens to you makes you take stock of and account for every aspect of your life.

I went up into this quiet little room with a kindly old gentleman, my auditor. He said there wasn't any reason to get into anything heavy right away, but we needed to comprehensively cover a specific aspect of my life. I thought for a minute. I'd had an operation to remove my tonsils when I was about four, and thought it might be interesting to return to this.

He told me to go back to the beginning of the incident and run through it like it was happening all over again, right now. So I narrated exactly what had occurred, and told him I could really feel the pain in my throat. He said it was perfectly normal: 'Now we're going to go through the event again, and this time I want you to pick up any other additional information you can sense, like anything that was said by the doctors and staff working around you, how things smelled, things like that.'

He told me to return to the beginning of the event once more, to go through it again and tell him when I was done. I did so, picking up a few more details this time. When I was through, he asked me, 'How's that pain in your throat now?'

I thought for a minute. 'Yeah, it's still there . . . I can feel it like it just happened.'

'OK,' he said, 'we're going to go through it again – remember, try to recall anything else that happened.'

We did this once more and I noticed the pain had lessened by degree. A few more times, and I couldn't feel the pain any more. I could remember it vividly, but distance had been placed between myself and the experience. It had only taken about 45 minutes, but I now had an insight into how Dianetics actually worked.

I went back up to the city again at the end of the week, for another session. (I don't recall exactly what we addressed, probably some childhood injury – God knows I'd had enough of them.) At around this time a series of events began to occur in my personal life that put an end to my sessions in the city. It wouldn't be until four years later that it all became clear to me that these sessions were the first step towards waking up and coming out of the fog I'd been living in.

Now I was faced with what happened down at Ground Zero. Everything I'd seen. All the friends I'd lost. The movie replaying itself over and over in my head.

It was time to seek help again.

11

Toxic Fire

Another night tour in Ladder 4 – on a Friday night, no less. It was always crazy at the weekends. The front doors were open and, as usual, people were hanging around out front, talking with the firefighters, taking photos and buying company t-shirts. This place was at the heart of the city, and for every tourist who wanted to come and see Times Square and 42nd Street, there were others who now wanted to see the FDNY for themselves. Every time we went out on a fire run, there were half a dozen or more people taking pictures or shooting video cameras. It was like starring in an amateur movie every time we pulled out of the firehouse.

The clock read 1800 hours – time for roll call. I walked over to the front of the new firetruck, which replaced the brand new rig they had when I worked there on August 31. It had been about a week old back then, but was demolished down at the World Trade Center. Its replacement was exactly the same, with a computer screen up front and an alarm that rang like a telephone when notification of a run came in.

As I was writing the roll, I saw a list of the men who died down there. Carl Asaro's name stuck out for me. Carl had been the division chief's aide. I used to speak to him a few times a week to get my assignments. He had been a very witty guy and never missed a chance to break my chops. But he'd also go out of his way sometimes to help me in setting up a tour, or changing an assignment that didn't fit my schedule. I believe he was in Tower One when it came down, God rest his soul.

An announcement was made over the intercom, and everybody saddled up to head out. I climbed up into the cab of the rig. It was a massive ladder truck, with two huge outriggers on either side that put down when the 100-foot aerial ladder was utilised. Two big arms stuck out from the sides of the rig to hold it off the ground while it was held up in the front and the rear by hydraulic lifts, held firm with metal cotter pins. It all lifted the entire apparatus off the ground when the ladder was being used.

The chauffeur started the rig and the powerful engine roared to life. We pulled out of the firehouse as the public gaped and took pictures. As we cruised down the street, people waved and pretty girls made eyes at the guys in the back. The men just love it when that happens. The departmental radio was chattering in the background, but I hadn't yet heard of any fires tonight in Manhattan. Still, we knew that, out of the five boroughs of New York City, there was usually a fire in progress every hour or so in at least one borough. Sometimes there were more.

The rig was parked and the guys piled out to get whatever was needed for the meal that evening, leaving me listening out for any calls sent via the computer. I was alone with my thoughts. My cousin, Sean Sweeney, was going to Northern Ireland for the thirtieth anniversary of Bloody Sunday at the end of January. I would have liked to go with him, but I couldn't swing it with the Department. It would be a sombre commemoration of another tragic event, but I felt that, as NYC firefighters, we could have offered moral support.

I'd spoken to Sean last night after dinner at my mom's – the first time I'd seen him since before the 11th. He told me how he'd been down at the scene on the morning of the 12th, about 6 a.m. and worked until dark, following the same routine for a week. The horrors found by him, the firefighters and the police were almost indescribable: there was a woman's face on the ground, like a mask with no eyes, the skin torn right off her skull; a pregnant woman was pulled dead from beneath the ruins.

'We were up on the Pile,' Sean told me, 'way up on the top of it, over off on the Liberty Street side. It took some doing to get up there, and we were handing shit out in a line to search some voids down below. I turned and saw this firefighter. He was kinda old looking, he might have been a retired guy, and he was looking a little lost. He looked at me with tears in his eyes and said, "Can I stay here? Is it all right if I just stay here for a bit?" I just said, "Yeah, buddy. It's gonna be OK." He just sat down on a beam with a faraway look in his eyes.'

Back at the firehouse, people were still turning up in droves. We backed in and shut the door. The guys had got a meal to prepare, and every once in a while they needed a break from all the people who wanted to come in and talk about it. 'Where were you on the day? I was doing *blah, blah, blah* at the time, and I saw it on TV, and *Oh my God*!...' – though it truthfully didn't bother me. Other people needed to talk about it too. Everyone had been affected by what happened, in some way, shape or form.

I went back into the office to get some paperwork done. I was only sitting down for about a minute when the alarm bells rang. The house watchman was immediately on the intercom, 'Everybody get out! Fire on the second floor, 243 West 44th Street!'

We were all aboard in less than thirty seconds and blasting our way down 48th Street, lights flashing and sirens wailing down to Broadway where we made a right. There were a lot of cars stopped at the red light up ahead. I dispensed with them with a very loud, very powerful new air horn. We made the turn on to 44th Street and my eyes were scanning the addresses.

Up ahead there was someone in the middle of the street, waving us in. My heart rate immediately doubled. Other people stood out front, having recently evacuated, some holding themselves with their arms folded across their chests.

I climbed down out of the rig with my mask straps loosely hanging over the front of my chest. I leaned over, shifting the weight of the mask up to the middle of my back and cinched up the straps so the mask sat properly on my shoulders. The can man – a firefighter armed with a portable extinguisher – and forcible entry man were right behind me.

As I headed into the lobby, people were streaming past me. 'It's right on the next floor!' someone shouted. As I headed up the stairs, I reached around and cracked open the valve that lets air into the mechanism on my mask, so that I could don the face-piece when I needed to. I hit the second floor and saw smoke down the hall, getting a good look at the layout to see how far I could go before I had to put my mask on.

I transmitted the signal to the chief out in the street, telling him we had a working fire. Smoke puffed out from a small, closet-like foyer. The smoke was extremely acrid, and I was forced down to the floor where I fumbled with my face-piece to get some clean air into my lungs.

I tried the door but it was locked, and hot to the touch. The forcible entry man was right behind me, but he didn't have his mask on and was probably taking a feed from all the smoke spewing out from around the edge of the door.

There was almost zero visibility, so I took my mask off to see more clearly. Bad move. This was really shitty smoke, leaving a bitter taste in my mouth and throat. I fumbled around, trying to see how the door opened. The chief was calling me on my radio. I couldn't answer him because I couldn't breathe. I frantically pressed the mask to my face to take a quick breath before I passed out. I lay down low on the floor and told the chief we were working on the door, acting as his eyes while he was out on the street.

The forcible entry man was working his tool into the slim space between the jamb and the door. The engine company was right next to me with the hoseline, hunkered down low until they were needed. But, in the back of my mind, the worst scenario was beginning to unfold – if we didn't get the door open soon, the fire would be that much harder to extinguish, possibly driving us back out on to the staircase.

The forcible entry man got the door open and the smoke enveloped him, pushing him out into the hallway, darkening everything, turning the whole place into night. The engine officer called for water to the guy out in the hall, manning the hoseline connected to the building's water main.

The can man was right behind me as we crawled into the room to locate the fire. The heat was starting to bank down, and it was getting very hot just a few feet above the floor. The forcible entry man yelled back to me, 'Hey Lou, there's hazardous materials in here!' We backed out of the room and shut the door behind us. There were two-gallon containers lined up inside the door with labels warning that they contained corrosives. I transmitted this information to the chief, who very calmly told me to make sure we kept our masks on.

We re-entered the room, spreading out to locate the source of the fire. 'It's over here, Lou!' the other two guys yelled to me from the right-hand side. I headed in the direction of their voices, fumbling in the darkness as objects fell down around my head. I could hear the can being sprayed as well as the crackling of flames up ahead.

'Where are you guys?' I screamed, taking my mask off for a brief instant. Man, that smoke was bad. 'Right over here,' came a voice right in front of me. But I still couldn't see them, or even see the flames.

Finally, I caught a glimpse of the jet of water from the extinguisher can's nozzle. The stream was illuminated by the flames on the other side of the room. I couldn't make out what was burning, and I heard the engine officer yelling out, 'Where's the fire?' – but it still seemed to me we were getting a handle on it.

I pulled my face-piece off for a brief instant to yell, 'Over here!' and shone my flashlight. The engine crawled over to where we were. I told my guys to hold their positions and headed back towards where I believed the front door was. I could see that it was starting to clear up a bit, and that the second truck was searching the other side of the fire area. It looked like we were in some kind of factory or workshop. I went back to where I'd told the guys to stay. We waited for a few more minutes while the engine shot several hundred gallons of water into the area that was burning.

The fire was out now, and the intense heat was fading – I knew this because I could see a few guys from Rescue standing up straight and talking to each other in full voice. They weren't wearing their masks, so I thought it was OK to do the same.

Big mistake.

As soon as I took a few lungfuls of that awful smoke, my throat closed up and began to burn. I immediately pushed my face-piece on, desperately in need of clean air.

The guys from Rescue go to so many fires that they become accustomed to breathing in some of that crap. I was not as well conditioned, and a few inhalations really knocked me for a loop. I kept my mask on for a little while longer, until almost all of the smoke had lifted. It was too late to protect myself, however, and I was having a little trouble breathing.

As the smoke cleared up, I began to look around at where we were. At first I thought it was a photo shop, because there were all these sinks that looked like darkroom sinks. Then I saw the sign on the door that said 'Foundry'. It was a jewellery factory, where they made all their little plastic moulds. Great – I'd been breathing in burning plastic.

The chief came up and told me to take my guys down to the street for a break. When I got down there, I wasn't feeling too good. I sat down on the bumper of the rig and, after a while, began to feel a little better. Then I had one very major coughing attack. Combined with what I was already experiencing as a result of the WTC fires, it had me starting to worry.

That night, when we got back, I went into the bathroom and hacked up what looked like caviar – little globules that looked just like black roe. This went on for the rest of the week. Each time I spat up, I was afraid to look at what colour it was. It took a week before it lightened from black to the familiar yellowish tone I'd become accustomed to, and which hadn't left my chest since September 11.

When I arrived home the next morning, I went into the bathroom and had a coughing attack which woke up the baby and my wife. She came up to me and said, 'John, you've got to do something about your health.' I knew she was right. I had been putting off doing something about my situation for too long now. I told her that I would do something tomorrow... promise. She was OK with what I told her but I felt her doubt shining through her acknowledgement.

12

Dealing with Anthrax

It was a night tour at Ladder 2, located on 51st street on the east side of Midtown. Lately, there had been a lot of calls to do with anthrax. Suspicious envelopes, white powder, strange smell, you name it. It came in all shapes and sizes; according to the calls. At the beginning of the tour, I was praying that we wouldn't have to deal with anything like that. In addition, I had already made my mind up that if we did I wouldn't be letting my men go into the building. I briefed them at roll call and we were all in agreement on this point. We would evacuate people and give them first aid, but other than that, we would stay put until units arrived who were better equipped to handle this sort of stuff.

I guess I was signing my own death warrant in hoping for a quiet night. Right after I finished writing the roll, a call came in over the teleprinter. I was sitting right next to it and I watched as, rather ominously, the paper rolled out and over the back of the printer. I could clearly see ANTHRAX THREAT... The address and all the particulars followed. It really grabbed my attention, you could say.

The house watchman jumped into the room and read off the details over the loudspeaker. Immediately, the firehouse was swarming with firefighters, hustling into their turnout gear. The 8th battalion is stationed in this firehouse alongside Ladder 2 and Engine 8. The battalion chief tonight happened to be Jack Mooney, and he was out on the apparatus floor greeting us as we turned out.

The chief addressed us all as one: 'OK guys, when we get to the location, nobody goes up on the floor where the package was reported to be! We will assist anyone who needs to come down to the street and will help the hazardous materials unit or Squad when they arrive.' Everyone agreed with him. After all, he was the boss. We mounted up and out the door we went. To who knew what?

As we moved down the street, I was thinking to myself about how terrible things had become here in New York, with all these anthrax threats. The news didn't help, sensationalising every last bit of it. Sometimes it seemed like the news was worse than what had really happened.

Threats were coming in all over the city. Sometimes, there would be two or three of them at once, tying up all the resources of the emergency services. It was extremely frustrating that nothing could be done to catch whoever was committing these heinous acts. Almost all of the threats were false alarms, but the few real incidents that did occur kept us on edge. Another time it could have driven guys over the edge, but nothing compared to what had happened on the 11th. You could say we were seasoned in the horror department by now. We all continued to do our jobs. That was our hallmark.

As we arrived at the scene, there was a group of civilians gathered in front of the building. Some were holding handkerchiefs over their noses as they exited the front doors. It looked like the real McCoy. I got off the rig as the driver pulled it over to the kerb, angling it to protect us from the traffic that continued to stream by us as we exit the apparatus. No one wastes any time here in New York. I approached the crowd of people standing in front of the building. One of them said, 'It's in the elevator shaft! Anthrax in the elevator shaft! That's what the note said, that I found on my desk!'

I gave my report to Chief Mooney. 'Ladder 2 to Battalion 8 . . . '

'Battalion 8, go with your message.'

'We have reports of an envelope with anthrax in it in the elevator shaft.'

'Ten-four, Ladder 2.'

'Let's cordon off the area, and be sure to not let anyone into the building'

I gave a closing ten-four and my guys encircled the building with yellow hazardous materials tape so people would be alerted as to what was going on.

All of this really pissed me off. Was there really a package in the elevator shaft? Or was it someone's idea of a sick joke? It wasn't the first time I'd come across something like that. Some people make a career out of doing that kind of thing.

So we stood out in the street and stopped anyone from coming into the building. Haz-Mat, the hazardous materials unit, eventually arrived about fifteen minutes later and took control of the situation. These guys wore fully encapsulated suits, like space suits, that would protect them from anthrax spores. They went in and after forcing open the elevator doors, found a package of white powder at the base of the shaft. It was packaged and sealed in a special drum and then taken away for testing.

Listening to the transmissions between the officer of Haz-Mat and the Division chief, who had assumed control of the whole operation by now, it came to me: this was a really screwed-up situation for the hazardous materials guys to be in. What if something happened to their gear while they were operating? What if they then became exposed? All in the line of duty.

It stank. But we were all just doing our job.

13

Addressing My Health

I wake up coughing and I can't stop. My wife nudges me to go into the bathroom before I wake the baby. Closing the door, I get another uncontrollable coughing fit that lasts for about a minute. While coughing so hard, I throw my back out. Man, now I'm really a mess. I go to open the door and another fit of coughing comes over me. After that, I sit on the tub and think to myself, what the hell did I breathe in down there? I've been a firefighter for seventeen-plus years and have never suffered like this. A lot of guys are out with respiratory problems, I know that. But I can't afford to go on medical leave. I need to earn money on a moonlight job and you're not allowed to work while you're on medical leave.

I'd been thinking about a health regimen that was available at Scientology churches in New York, called the purification rundown. L Ron Hubbard created it back in the sixties due to the amount of drug use he was finding among people who came to the church seeking help.

The purification rundown is based on the theory that a person's body can become like a toxic waste dump after years of exposure to drugs – not just street drugs but pesticides, preservatives and all the other contaminants that we ingest throughout our lives. The programme focuses on the toxins that have become lodged in your body's fatty tissues. It involves aerobic exercise followed by sitting in a sauna to sweat out the toxins which have been released into the bloodstream. This is combined with a healthy diet, lots of water and vitamins. This type of cleansing process was followed by the

Romans, the Scandinavians and the Russians. The difference with Hubbard's programme is the emphasis on vitamins and a good diet.

As a firefighter, I'm trained to put my mask on to protect myself from the hazards of breathing in the noxious substances we come in contact with. However, we don't always put our masks on right away. They cut down your vision. You often wait until you start moving in with the hose before you put your mask on, so you can see where you're going for the few brief instants before it all goes black.

In addition, in the later stages of a fire, after all of the visible flames are extinguished and the incident is under control, guys tend to take their masks off. It's natural and we all do it. It makes it easier to see what you're doing.

Now, after seventeen years on the job, I've become a strong advocate of keeping your mask on. The amount of toxins that you can inhale in just a few moments is staggering. A lot of these poisons are deposited in your fatty tissues for ever.

I'd completed the programme once before. At that time I had already been on the Fire Department about eleven years and had ingested a lot of toxins from the green smoke at car fires and the various other materials that you feel are of no harm. Now I was thinking about doing it again, after what I'd been exposed to down at the Trade Center disaster. Maybe it would help my cough.

Around this time there were a lot of guys, maybe four hundred, out on medical leave – due, I suppose, to whatever they'd breathed in down at Ground Zero. There wasn't much being done for them and I thought that perhaps the Hubbard programme could be set up in the New York Fire Department. Hey, if I could get a few guys to do it with me I wouldn't be so lonely in the sauna.

The next morning I called a friend who knew a bit more about the place out in California that delivers the purification programme. The clinic is called Health Med, and I checked out their website. The doctor running it was a retired Air Force colonel by the name of David Root. He was loaded with credentials and he'd been using the programme for twenty years, putting over three thousand people through it.

I was sure some of my fellow firefighters who were sick might benefit from such a programme under medical supervision. At least the guys could do something proactive about it. So I found the phone number for an organisation known as FASE (Foundation for Advancements in Science and Education) They had participated in numerous published research reports on the detoxification programme in the past and Dr David Root was a senior associate of the foundation. When I contacted them they were very interested in what I had to say, and promised to send me some literature so that I could show it to the fire department's chief medical officers and unions.

It's a tough job to bring changes to, or introduce anything new. The guys always figure that there's an angle to whatever's being shoved in their faces, and often there probably is. But one thing was for sure. The only vested interest I had was in seeing that these guys who were sick got a chance to have this programme.

I was off the phone now, alone with my thoughts. My wife Tami came into the room. 'Who was that you were speaking to?'

I told her all about what just transpired. She looked excited; she exclaimed, 'Oh wow, that sounds like a great idea.'

Yeah, I thought to myself, this is a great idea, but it's going to take a lot of hard work to get it implemented. First there are the doctors, then there's the money, and where it's going to be done. It looks insurmountable. But I'm just going to take it one step at a time.

The next day I called up the union rep in charge of firefighters' health issues. His name is Thomas Manley and I used to work with him once in a while when I was a firefighter in Brooklyn. I briefly explained to him about the purification programme but I could tell he wasn't really listening. I asked what was up. He explained that he was on his way to a funeral, one of many that were taking place that day. Send me something to read, he said. Knowing some literature was being sent to me from the Health Med people, I agreed. He suggested I should call him in about a week, after he had read what I sent him.

I had to work in Ladder 4 that night and my back was still in pretty bad shape. I lay down for a while on the living room floor to see if it would straighten out. Every once in a while this happened to me – I'd been to the chiropractor a long time ago – but it hadn't been this bad for a long time. Being in the heart of Midtown Ladder 4 is generally a very busy place. In addition to that it was a Friday night and I knew there would be no rest for the weary. I lay on the rug of the living room, my wife off at work and the baby with the sitter, and contemplated calling in sick. I rolled over on to my stomach. Hmm, that wasn't too bad, perhaps something shifted. By now it was nearly time to leave, so I decided to tough it out and make the best of it.

Arriving at Ladder 4, I took the working officer's gear off the rig and replaced it with mine, putting his away. I told the house watchman to let the boss know he was up. (That's what we say in this job. 'You're up' means you can leave.) I made my way to the office in the back of the apparatus floor. It was empty; the officer was probably working out downstairs in the gym. Sitting down at the desk, I looked at the evening's riding list. I was familiar with everyone on the list and that gave me a comfortable feeling.

The daytime officer entered the room,

'Hey John, how's it going?'

'As good as can be expected.'

'Same here.'

He handed me the riding list from the day as the tour wasn't over yet. 'Got to run.'

'Fine, I got it.'

He grabbed his bag and left. He was a covering officer himself, living out of a carry bag, never knowing where he'd be working until the day before, and sometimes not until the last minute.

A firefighter came into look at the day book, to see who was on duty so he could fill in the journal on the watch. He took a few minutes to do this, saying, 'I'll just be a minute, Lou, and then I'll be out of your way.'

'Take your time,' I said, 'I'm here for the night.'

Once he found the names he was off again. On the file cabinets were seven picture frames containing photos of the missing guys from this company. I took a quick look at them. I'd worked with every one of them at some point or another over the past three years. So much experience, gone forever. These were all seasoned fire-fighters, who could be counted on to get the job done. You can't put a price on that; it's numbing to look at all the faces. I stopped looking; it was pulling my attention away from where it should be, which was right here and now.

When the bells rang for the change of tours I headed out to the front of the apparatus floor, where the men assemble. With the riding list for the night in my head I asked the senior man what he thought was this evening's best line-up. Taking the list, he wrote down the names before handing it back to me. I looked it over, giving each man his assignment for the night. Then I was off to the house watch to write the roll call.

It was now 11 p.m. We were coming back from our fifth run of the night – busy enough to keep you on your toes. The rig stopped in front of the firehouse and I stepped down from the big front cab on to the street. We were blocking four lanes of traffic with the rig, which is the norm when it's backing in.

As I stepped down, I felt a sharp pain in my back and I realised that I couldn't walk. This was serious! I was standing in the middle of Eighth Avenue and I couldn't walk.

I started to take baby steps, hoping it didn't look too obvious. I asked one of the guys to give me a hand. Christ, I was thinking, I'm like an old man. Now I was definitely thinking about going out sick. Tommy Clinton helped me a little, saying, 'Hey Lou, you all right?'

I reached the kerb, and began to feel a little better. Then again that pain! I managed to get back to my office, holding my breath for most of the way. But I wasn't going to let this get the best of me. I sat down on the floor and did some stretching, touching my knees, then my toes. I'd done this before and it seemed to help. Standing up I decided to sit in the easy chair; it was easier to get out of. After a while in the chair, I dozed off.

We had another run about an hour and a half later. Amazingly, I was able to get up and out without too much trouble. I had my gear on, so there was minimal bending. We were all aboard the rig and screaming up Eighth Avenue in no time. The run turned out to be just a faulty alarm, so I gave the signal over the Deparment radio and we headed for home.

The rest of the night was pretty uneventful. There were a few more nonsense runs but I managed a solid three hours sleep between

5 a.m. and 8 a.m. I went home and lay down, hoping my back would get better as I had to go in again for my second night tour. That's the way it goes when you're covering: two night tours, 72 hours off, two day tours, 48 hours off. A night tour is from 6 p.m. to 9 a.m. the next morning, a day tour is from 9 a.m. to 6 p.m. Sometimes you can work 24-hour tours, swapping your night for a day with a guy that's opposite you. But for me right now, that wasn't the deal.

Unable to get any more sleep, I tossed and turned in bed. I'd reached my threshold of pain and decided to call in sick. After that I took two aspirins and sat on the couch thinking. There wasn't much that I could do in the shape I was in. Perhaps the best thing for me to do was nothing.

Sometime during the day, I went out to check the mail, and was pleasantly surprised to find the information from Health Med had already arrived. I opened it up and looked it over. There was an article about a bunch of firefighters from Shreveport, Louisiana who were flown to the clinic and went through the detoxification programme. These firefighters were exposed to PCBs (poly-chlorinated biphenels, a known carcinogen) and had significant health problems after their exposure.

The article went into minute details about how the programme cleaned these guys up and returned them to full duty status. All kinds of statistics were provided. The article had been published in *Fire Engineering*, back in '87. I wondered to myself, why couldn't this be integrated into the NYC Fire Department as a sort of maintenance? We've got self-contained breathing apparatus and we're trained to put it on, but there are always situations where you're exposed to smoke. I was scheduled to report to the medical office tomorrow and I needed to make copies to take to the chief medical officer.

The next day, I reported to the medical office, having made copies on the way for the two doctors. I was seen by one of the regular clinic doctors, who asked me how I was feeling. I explained the trouble I'd been having, adding that I should be OK to return to full duty for my next set of day tours. That would give me 72 hours to feel better, which should be enough. Then I raised the subject of the detoxification programme. He didn't seem to be too thrilled – I guess there must have been a thousand different suggestions coming at him and the rest of the medical staff every day from all over the world. But the difference between this programme and others, I insisted, is that this one gets results. It succeeds where others have failed, because it addresses the toxins that are stored in the fatty tissues. There is no other programme like it. When I told him this, he brightened a bit, but said he couldn't speak on behalf of his boss.

I explained what I was planning to do and he wished me good luck. Striaght away I was out the door, on my way to find the chief medical officer's secretary. I left the information with her, accompanied by a brief letter of introduction.

A week later I decided to call the doctor in charge of the medical division. Her secretary asked me to leave my number, so the doctor could return my call. I was surprised at this, considering how busy she must be, but only about an hour later the doctor herself called back. She hadn't looked at the literature I sent, but said she would now, after speaking to me. It was frustrating, but I could understand. Right now, every snake-oil salesman in the world had their eyes on the NYC Fire Department. Everybody had 'the solution' and most of the stuff was a lot of crap. But I was convinced that this could help our guys and vowed to myself not to give up.

The next week, in the daily news, there was a headline that read '200 Firefighters Out Sick'. I cut out the article. It featured Thomas Manley, the firefighters' union representative, talking about how many guys were currently out on medical leave with complications as a result of being exposed down at Ground Zero. After reading this, I was even more certain that Manley should be more involved in getting this programme to New York. I needed to get the purification info over to him and there was no more time to lose. I made some copies at the firehouse and mailed them out the next day.

A few days later, I called Tom and asked him if he'd received the info about the programme. He said yes, but he really didn't have any time to look at it. Once again, I was struck with the feeling that it was useless, that there was no way I was going to get this pro-gramme even looked at. But after we'd spoken for a while he told me to try and arrange a meeting between the Californian clinic and the chief medical officers.

Days passed by, funerals every day. Some sparsely attended, there were so many each day. Firehouses had to be manned by guys hired from other boroughs, because everyone was attending the funerals. We all wondered when it was going to quiet down a bit. It had been three months now and there were still funerals taking place, memorial services as well.

I went to a funeral service for the captain of Rescue 1. His name was Terry Hatton, he was a real tall guy, he had a real presence and he was very well respected. I'd come across him once at a fire on 9th Avenue, while I was working with Engine 54. His wake was being held on the Upper East Side of Manhattan, in a very smart funeral parlour.

I walked into the funeral parlour and was escorted upstairs, where Terry's wake was taking place. I went over to the casket. A helmet lay on top, with the words 'Rescue 1', on the front piece. After saying a prayer, I headed over to meet his parents and offer my condolences. His father took my hand and looked into my eyes. The depth of his pain was clearly visible in them and I held his gaze, trying to offer whatever solace I could. He wouldn't let go of my hand and so I told him the story of a fire I'd attended with his son.

I'd had a job with Engine 54 about a year ago. Ladder 4 entered the apartment and tried to put out the fire with the can but it flared up on them and they had to bail out of the room. It was all assholes and elbows in the hallway. The heat was intensifying and the fire was taking hold of the room again. I attempted to get my men in position to enter the apartment with the hoseline but the truck company was in the way. The guys hadn't given up trying to get in past the fire to do a search. We were all hunkered down low when all of a sudden a big booming voice was shouting orders. I looked up from down on the floor and it was Terry, larger than life. He said with complete authority, 'Hey, Ladder 4 ... move down the hall and let 54 by, so we can put out the fire, let's go!' The response from Ladder 4 was immediate and we had the fire under control in seconds.

His father was still holding my hand and I felt people starting to stare. But I really didn't give a shit. If I could make this man feel any better, it was worth more than any bad feelings I had to experience. He finally let go and introduced me to his wife. I gave her my condolences and stepped away, as the line to meet them was growing.

Usually after a wake or a funeral, there's a gathering for all to attend. I had gone to enough of these to know that I'd probably have a hangover the next morning. I went home to my wife and child. I hadn't spent any time with them for quite a while.

14

Fire's in the Mind

After telling my wife that I was going to get a grip on my health I knew I had to do something. That's how I found myself being interviewed by a lady at the Church of Scientology, on 82nd Street in Manhattan's Upper East Side. Having been there a few years back, I was familiar with some of the people who worked there. I had sat and talked before with this woman, right after I had gone through my divorce. I trusted her and was willing to listen to her advice.

So I told her how bad I'd been feeling lately and about all the coughing attacks, and we spoke a little about what happened on the 11th. She must have detected the grief stored inside me, because she asked me if I would be interested in getting help with it. She was referring to Dianetics counselling, but I didn't know if I was up to confronting what had happened just yet. I explained that I didn't know if I was ready for it, saying I was OK right now. I knew that was a bit of a lie, but I didn't feel comfortable asking for help. I knew that what I would be looking at would bring up a lot of pain and difficult memories.

She didn't let me off so easily, however. Once she'd asked me a few questions about the 11th, I realised before I knew it that I needed to do this for my own sanity and for the sake of my family. I told her I'd changed my mind and she said she would see what she could do about getting someone to help me.

I went home and slept a little better, knowing I was finally going to do something about myself. She called me later on, around 9 p.m., to tell me that I could be seen tomorrow around lunchtime, and that I should try to get a good night's rest. My wife was relieved to know that finally things would be addressed.

I managed to get a fair amount of sleep, in between bad dreams that woke me up a few times. I had a big breakfast and took my wife and baby to the park, where we let the little guy run through the grass and do his best at climbing trees. Man, he's going to be a handful, I thought to myself.

After bringing them home I headed off to the church to keep my appointment. When I arrived, I was given the royal treatment. I was escorted up to the top floor, to the small private rooms that are used to give counselling sessions.

I was already familiar with the procedure – I'd had it used on me with great results in the past – so I knew to how the whole things was run. And one of the drawbacks of a Dianetics session is that it can go on for a very long time – sometimes for three or more hours. So it can be very hard work not to mention the emotions that come up and the pain of reliving past upsets.

The woman who would be working with me was Jayne Kraman; it was she who'd called me a short time back offering her services. She welcomed me into the room and had me sit in a comfortable chair. After a little small talk, I begun to feel more comfortable with what we were about to do. She suggested that we ought to get started, and I agreed.

She asked me to shut my eyes and return to the morning of September 11, then gradually recall what happened. A few times along the way, I felt an overwhelming desire to cry. But I wasn't ready just yet; it didn't feel warranted. About an hour and a half later I'd finished running through the incident in my mind. I told Jayne that I was done. She then asked me to go through it all again.

I didn't feel very different. If anything, I felt a little worse.

'All right, we're going to do it again now. Are you at all hungry?'

'No.'

'Good, if you do get hungry, let me know and we'll stop for a break. OK?'

'Yeah.'

'Close your eyes again.' I do so. 'Now return to the beginning of the incident and tell me when you're there.'

I did so; it took another hour to recall the events of 9/11 and what has happened since again. This time through, I remembered a lot more details. When I got to the part where I was reading the sheets that listed who was missing, I couldn't hold it in any more. A tremendous feeling of grief came over me and I broke down weeping uncontrollably for about five minutes before I was able to carry on. I was silent for a bit and Jayne asked me if I was all right to continue. Gathering myself together, I told the remainder of the story. I let Jayne know I was finished. She said, 'Open your eyes.' I did so.

I was feeling a little better right now but I was still a bit frazzled. She suggested we take a break for something to eat and then see how I felt about continuing.

As I left the building to find a bite to eat, everything around me seemed a bit brighter and I felt a little less burdened. I walked down the street with a new sense of hope and for the first time since the events of 9/11, started thinking about paying my bills. I hadn't even looked at my mail, I'd been so consumed with what had occurred. It was all lying in a pile on my kitchen table. 'I'll do that tomorrow,' I said to myself. I guess we were making some progress.

After eating I returned to the room where Jayne was waiting. She wanted to know if I'd eaten.

'OK, how do you feel about continuing?' I thought about it for a minute. Damn, it takes such a long time to do this. But I was feeling better, perhaps I can feel better still. So, we began once again and three hours later, we were through for the night. I went home and for the first time since 9/11 had a pretty decent night's sleep, without any nightmares or interruptions.

The next morning I decided to go to the health food store and do some shopping. It was time to get back some of my good habits. Eating well was always one of my better habits but lately I'd taken to eating fast foods on a regular basis. At one time I swore I'd never again eat a Big Mac, but to my sorrow, I'd been unable to uphold this pledge.

After shopping, and a good healthy breakfast, I was off for another session. In contrast to many conventional therapies, Dianetics continues until you've dealt with whatever is being addressed. It's not 45 minutes once or twice a week. It deals with the matter at hand, from start to finish, addressing you as a spiritual being. That used to be a difficult concept for me. A 'spiritual being' – what the hell is that? Well, I understand it as your whole being. It's not your body, it's not your brain. It's you, purely and simply you.

I arrive at the townhouse on 82nd Street, where Jayne works. When I got up to her room, she was already there. 'How'd you sleep last night?' she asked.

I told her about my successful night's sleep. All she said was, 'Wow, imagine that.' She didn't sound too surprised. We do the same as yesterday and I was in session for about another five hours. There were more bouts of uncontrollable sobbing before, at the end of the day, something happened for me. It's hard to explain, but something shifted in my mind about how I viewed the whole thing.

It's personal and I've only shared what occurred with my auditor. But I know that before I wasn't doing too well and now everything looked different, I felt able to face the future with a healthier outlook.

Because of my personal experience, it now became a goal of mine to get other firefighters interested in Dianetics. We're trained in how to save lives but we need help to cope with emotional trauma that accompanies this – especially after an event on the scale of September 11. There's nothing worse than seeing one of your fellow workers totally distraught, or a grieving member stuck in their grief. Guys are often reluctant to seek help for emotional issues – it doesn't fit in with the firehouse culture.

After getting sorted out with the help of those few sessions, things around me began to look up. I took my bills to work my next set of tours and cleared them all. There was plenty of money available due to the overtime that I had worked over the past two months. All I had to do was mail some cheques and apologise to a few creditors, who quite understood about my delay in paying

When I spoke to my wife from the firehouse she insisted that I should start addressing my physical health. I got upset with her, we had an argument and she hung up the phone on me. When it came to helping myself, I still wasn't too fast to move.

I mulled over the thought of starting the programme. You weren't allowed to drink while doing it. Christmas was coming up and New

Years. There would be a party at my mom's house on Christmas Eve, it was always a good night to have a few drinks with all my family. Starting the programme meant that I would have to bite the bullet and give up alcohol.

But as I thought over what had transpired between my wife and me it became apparent that I would have some apologising to do when I came home in the morning and I would have to get started on this programme as soon as possible. I had three weeks' vacation coming. It would be a good time to jump into the health regimen. Maybe in three weeks' time I would be done.

15

Getting Healthy

It was my last night tour before I was to start my vacation. I was up on 125th Street in Engine 37, one of my favourite places to work. When I arrived no one was there; they had responded to a fire about fifteen blocks away. I thought I'd do the right thing, so I drove up to where they were working to see if the lieutenant who I was relieving wanted to go home.

When I arrived, I found that a dozen or more fire apparatus had responded. The street was full of hoses leading into a series of storefronts, from where smoke belched out of the broken front windows. It was pretty cold out, so cold that the water that leaked from the hose connections was freezing on the street, making everything slippery.

I managed to park my car about a block and a half away from the scene. I put on my fire gear and walked over to where the chiefs were all standing, coordinating the efforts of the troops who worked inside the burning buildings.

I asked one of the chiefs where Engine 37 was working. He looked at a board they had set up, indicating where each company was, and said, 'They're down in the basement of the furniture store'.

As I entered the store, I came across a truck company working with their gas-powered saw, cutting holes in the floor, searching for hidden pockets of fire and trying to relieve the basement of the pent-up heat and smoke that had accumulated down there. I pushed on past them and followed the hoseline through the store to a staircase at the rear. I didn't have a mask with me and it was starting to get shitty, I knelt down low where the air was clearer, and caught my

157

breath. I made it down the stairs and followed the hoseline in the dark until I found Engine 37.

Once I located the officer I told him I was his relief. Surprised to see me, he thanked me up and down for coming to the fire to relieve him as he had a long ride home. I handed him the keys to my car and he gave me his mask, which I took thankfully. He was gone in a flash and I turned to the matter at hand. I looked around me; most of the guys were wearing their masks. The worst of the blaze had been extinguished and the truck company was opening up the ceiling to check for hidden pockets of fire. The next-door room where they were working was still thick with smoke.

I pushed my face-piece to my face and inhaled deeply. Ahhhh, fresh air. Then I donned the whole thing. I had consumed enough crap in the last few months and was tired of all the hacking that came with it.

Soon we were needed with the hoseline again to extinguish a fire that had suddenly flared up after the truck companies opened up the ceiling. We made short order of what was showing and once again, the place became dark around us, enveloping us in smoke. It cleared up in a few moments and I took my mask off to see more. At once I took a hit of smoke and broke out in a huge coughing fit. I quickly donned my face-piece once more to avoid ingesting any more toxins.

We worked for another twenty minutes or so, extinguishing the last vestiges of embers found in the smoking debris. A short while after that we were up and out in the street. It was great to breathe in the cold fresh winter air, and I promptly went into another coughing attack, unable to stop until I got up whatever was lining my throat.

Back at the firehouse, I went into the bathroom and spat into the toilet. Black. That was the colour. My wife called just at that moment and again raised the topic of when was I going to partake in the sauna programme that I'd been touting so heavily. The way she put it made it very hard for me to continue to avoid. After she'd shot down all of my excuses I finally gave in and agreed with her to start at the beginning of my vacation – which was the next day. I should have been happy to have a wife that cared that much for me. I'll have to work on that.

*

It was the end of the first week of December. My vacation had started today, and keeping to my word I showed up at the Scientology organisation to start the purification programme. I wasn't very eager to get started. I knew what would be ahead of me: a lot of sweating and days of not feeling my best due to what I had to go through to relieve my body of what I had ingested.

The facilities had recently been updated. The bathroom and shower were new and everything was clean and tiled white. It seemed like a nice environment to do something like this in, especially bearing in mind it was in the middle of New York City. There was a little backyard with plants and a place to sit while you took your breaks from the sauna.

I met the person in charge; Jolli Brown was her name. She would be there throughout the time I spent on the programme, ensuring that I was given everything I needed. She directed me to the changing rooms and told me to go and put on my jogging clothes. Man, she wasn't wasting any time. I was dreading the running that started you out each day.

I weighed in and took a range of vitamins. Before I knew it, I was on the treadmill, running for the obligatory twenty minutes before going into the sauna. One of the vitamins that you take is niacin, a 'B' vitamin. Niacin contributes to getting the toxins in the fatty tissues moving into the blood stream, from where they are brought to the eliminatory channels of the body. You take it a little at a time as your body can only sweat out so much poison in one go. While this is occurring, it's not very comfortable. But the days go by, and the amount of niacin you take is increased, sooner or later you begin to get used to it.

The run was pure torture. I hated running, plain and simple. I don't mind running up six flights of stairs to put out a fire, but treadmill running is boring and hard. When my twenty minutes were up I was instructed to 'Get into the box now.' That's what they call the sauna. I went in and sat down, it was hot as hell in there. A few minutes later, I began to sweat profusely; I could feel the niacin starting to take effect. After about twenty minutes, I had what felt like a mild sunburn all over my body, a reaction from the niacin.

There was a gallon of spring water at hand and I wasted no time in taking a healthy swig. I could take a break whenever I wanted to, or a

cool shower. It was tough, but I was resigned to seeing the programme through to the end. I had three weeks set aside to do just this.

While I was in the sauna, I often felt overwhelmed and was
unable to think clearly, I just had to sit there and sweat. It took some
hanging in there; it wasn't easy and at times I felt like nodding off.
There was sea salt to take, as well as potassium tablets which helped
stave off the feelings of tiredness and exhaustion. I'd take these as
often as I felt I needed them.

After a while, the feeling of exhaustion would go away and a
sense of relief would replace it, like I'd just got rid of something
bad. When the first day drew to an end, I felt overjoyed to take a
shower and head home.

But after a few days I was handling the regimen much better. It's
not for the faint of heart and takes a bit of doing before you get used
to it, but when you do, you can sit in the sauna and read to your
heart's content, catch up on all of the cheap love stories that you've
been putting aside. I spent my idle time doing crossword puzzles
and reading novels.

The days flew by. Before I knew it my vacation was over and I
was back in the firehouse. I'd been on the programme about four
weeks. One night, we responded to a fire. It had come in as a fire in
a bedroom in a residential multiple dwelling. When we showed up
there were a lot of people in the lobby. It looked like we had
something, so we made our way up the stairs to the fifth floor where
we started to smell smoke. We were the second due ladder company
and were assigned to the fire floor. As we headed up the stairs, the
smoke was getting thicker, and my the first thought was, I'm going
to ruin all the work I've been doing in the sauna by taking a feed at
this fire. I decided to put my mask on well ahead of time to avoid
taking in any smoke.

We made it up the stairs and into the area where all the smoke
was coming from. The first due ladder company, Ladder 13, was
there. They had almost extinguished the fire with their
extinguisher can and we helped in searching the huge five-room
apartment. The situation wasn't as bad as it first appeared and the
chief, who was on the fire floor watching what was going on, had
the fire under control.

I still kept my mask on. But I was starting to get stares from some of the guys so I took it off. The air was relatively clear by now but I wanted to avoid taking in any unnecessary smoke if it was at all possible.

That night proved not to be busy but I was surprised to wake up about seven the next morning, feeling refreshed and ready to face the day. I seemed to be needing less sleep than I usually required. Even though we had been at the fire and had to run up all those stairs and everything else that was involved, I just wasn't tired. A new sense of energy had seemed to come over me in the last few days that I had been on the programme. I was starting to think that I was done. I wrote this on the daily report that asks you to write down how the day went.

The day after that I was a little annoyed to see that Jolli Brown didn't agree. Once again, I dressed in my shorts and climbed on to the treadmill.

Now I had been on this regimen for about four weeks at that point in time. Although I was feeling considerably better, something happened that lengthened my stay.

Something started coming out of my eyes. Gunk started oozing from the corners of both my eyes, after I'd been in the sauna for about an hour each day. I'd have to wipe them every half hour or so or the gunk would just film over my eyeballs, making it hard to see. This continued for the next ten days or so, getting worse at one point. Eventually it began tapering off until finally it stopped. But I wasn't finished with the programme yet.

I was working at Ladder 13. It was a Sunday night and it shouldn't be too busy, but one could never tell around this part of town. The area covered by this firehouse has maybe the widest range of buildings anywhere in the city. This makes it a challenge to the firefighters who work here: every situation is different and each of the buildings they respond to is unique in some way.

After I wrote the roll call I went into the kitchen where the men began breaking my balls soundly. This was a good sign. It's when nobody says anything to you that you should begin to worry. I was just about to pour a cup of water – I was still sweating from being in the sauna all day – when the alarm bells went off. 'Everybody goes' came over the intercom, and we all headed out the kitchen door to the rigs. I jumped into my gear and the chauffeur started up the rig. 'Where are we going?' he shouted over the noise of the motor. I carefully looked at the ticket and gave him the address.

We were headed to a tenement about four blocks away. I knew this because information on the bottom of the ticket informs us of any special hazards that may present themselves in the building. The ticket stated, 'converted tenement into duplex apartments' and the fire was reported to be in a kitchen on the fifth floor. Opening the little window between myself and the guys in the back, I shouted to them, 'It says on the ticket that there are duplex apartments.'

When we arrived on the scene, nothing obvious was going on – no one was in the street, no smoke was coming out of any windows. Me and my team headed inside to investigate. I had all my gear on, mask, boots, helmet, jacket and coat, plus a small tool to pry things open and a flashlight. The other guys, with more to carry, were a tad behind me as I bounded up the stairs two at a time to the fifth floor. I was feeling very strong – maybe all that time in the sauna was beginning to pay off. I wasn't even out of breath. At this point in the regimen I had worked up to doing two nine-minute miles before I went into the sauna. Not bad for my 41-year-old body. I recalled when I first started. The run at the beginning was a horror, just doing a mile was a nightmare. I had come a long way in four weeks.

On the fifth floor, there was nothing showing. I went to the apartment indicated on the ticket and gave a bang on the door. 'I'll be right there,' came a voice from inside. I caught the smell of something burning on the stove. It has a distinct smell that's always the same. An elderly woman opened the door; now I could really smell it and there was a little haze in the apartment. But I could see that she already had put the burnt pot in the sink. Everything was OK. I transmitted the information to the chief down in the street, and we opened a few windows for the old lady. She was very thankful and said, 'God bless you guys, you're the best,' as we left her apartment.

When we got back to the firehouse, the guys cooked. I spent about an hour doing paperwork in the office until the call 'Chow's on!' came over the intercom. After eating I once again retired to the office to handle my paperwork. The guys were busy cleaning the kitchen, as is always the case after dinner. After a while I heard shouting out on the apparatus floor, in the back where there's a basketball hoop set up. I looked to see what was going on and was amazed to find eight of the guys pushing themselves around in these office chairs, playing basketball. It was something to see – just like watching the handicapped players in their wheelchairs. It looked pretty comical – some of the guys were a lot better at it than others – but the best thing was that they looked like they had put the misery behind themselves for a while. Nine guys had perished here and every day was a tough one. I smiled and went back to my paperwork.

The rest of the night was uneventful and I was happy to get a good six hours of rest in between runs that night. But I still had to go home and get some rest to be ready for another day in the sauna.

A few days later, though, I hit my finish point in the programme, now able to withstand staying in the box for extended periods of time, with no adverse effects. Instead, there was a feeling of being renewed, like I had regained my health and vitality as a firefighter. I told Jolli that I was finally done. It had taken me 40 days to achieve this. I got out of the box and showered with a sense of achievement, knowing that I would now feel better as a result of the steps I had taken to improve my health.

All I could hope for was that others, once informed, would also take advantage of this regimen.

16

After September 11

I came out of the Manhattan side of the Brooklyn Battery Tunnel on to West Street. Usually, I take the East Side drive uptown to where I live, but tonight I was drawn to take the West Side drive that had only recently been reopened. That route would take me directly through Ground Zero – the first time I'd driven that way in my car since before September 11. It was now late May 2002, more than eight months later.

I was waiting at the light one block before Liberty Street, wondering how I might react to what I saw.

I got up to Liberty Street, and passed underneath the walkway – nothing. I continued up West Street, recalling the huge hills of steel and debris that had littered the streets for the first month or so.

It was all gone.

All that remained of the World Trade Center was a huge, empty pit. It had a sort of vacant, antiseptic feeling to it. Lights shone down into the bottom of the pit; firefighters were still sifting through the dirt and the last remnants of whatever remained.

It was going to be hard for a lot of guys to leave this place, after all the work was done. They had been down there for a long time, working endless hours, volunteering during their time off out of a sense of brotherhood. They were the glue that held the job together throughout its darkest hour.

I'd stopped down there to volunteer about one month previously, continuing my stint long after the FDNY had put us all back on normal duties. Many guys there were volunteers, from all walks of life. We had spent the night raking through the final loads of debris.

Nothing was found, but, a few nights prior to this, they had found the mortal remains of several cops.

I passed the stop light at Vesey Street and drove on past the Verizon building. It was all a memory to me now, coloured by the dark smoke of gloomier days. I could look back, and no longer be a hostage to that terrible fear, pessimism and hopelessness. It will never lessen the importance of the events of September 11, but what occurred that day will no longer live rent-free in some dark corner of my mind.

If it all happened again tomorrow, only certain aspects would change. There would be better organisation, that's for sure, and not as many firefighters' deaths. But the dedication and selfless devotion would still be there. The guys who ran into those buildings are on a par with the soldiers who stormed the beaches of Normandy on D-Day, who, for the sake of what is right and just, sacrificed themselves so that others might live. There is no greater sacrifice than this.

Throughout the millennia, self-sacrificing soldiers have as often been the defenders against tyranny as its pawns. It's my belief that, while not engaged in battle against any external enemy, the emergency services of our modern world, the firefighters, paramedics and police, can sometimes harness the age-old warrior spirit in defence of their fellow human beings.

Things on 'the job' will never be the same. I'm sure that 9/11 will be looked upon as a demarcation line, when the job had to begin all over again in a new way. Running into burning buildings was always in a day's work. But now, it will always be accompanied by feelings of uncertainty, the feeling that we might not know what lurks behind an otherwise familiar scenario. 'Is this a trap to lure us into a building, where a secondary fire or explosion is going to kill us all?' This is the new attitude that we, as New York City firefighters, will have to live with from here on in.

The celebrity status we were all having a hard time with is now starting to fade. Many things are getting back to the way they were pre-9/11. I remember distinctly how the people of New York were beginning to treat one another differently, with more kindness and respect. As time has worn on, the soft veil of ignorance has descended once again. We are more insular, more concerned with our own petty problems. It's a microcosmic version of it, but it mirrors the blissful ignorance that existed up until that fateful morning – a failure to empathise with the other peoples of this world.

What happened that morning should be looked upon as a wake-up call, letting America and the rest of the world know all is not well on Planet Earth. We were told that the retaliatory attacks on Afghanistan were necessary, to show aggressors that they will not be tolerated, and show the world to what lengths America will go to protect her freedom. This is a matter of viewpoint. Throughout the history of humankind, no lasting peace was ever sustained by victory in war alone. Until we all acknowledge the seriousness of our situation, it's very apparent that humanity is coming ever closer to extinction. This urgently needs to be recognised by destructive fools like the zealots who planned the atrocities of September 11, even more than by the rest of us.

Truth, justice, freedom – these are fine principles, and the Constitution of my country is sworn to uphold them. However, even our largely free society is not without the kind of blinkered prejudice that led the fanatics of September 11th to believe they could commit mass murder justifiably, in the name of a God and a culture they felt to be inarguably superior to that of others. But I ask you to remember the men who ran into the burning towers that morning, to evacuate everyone that they could. They held no prejudices at all about anyone they might be able to save.

At the time of the publication of this book, the anniversary of September 11 will be upon us. I'm sure it will recur all over again in a lot of people's minds, particularly those who lost loved ones. It seems that the date now looms large in how we think and how we plan our lives. For those of us in the Fire Department, caring for the families of our brotherhood has become a part of our everyday affairs. But the responsibility to do likewise will be borne by everyone in some way, somehow. As the years roll on, the most positive effect that the events of 9/11 can have is that we recognise we all share the common purpose of caring for one another.

I can only hope that the compassion shown by my brothers in the Fire Department on that fateful day will be an example to others in the years to come.

I'm proud to have served with you.